Palgrave Studies in Creativity and Culture

Series editors
Vlad Petre Glăveanu
Department of Communication and Psychology
Aalborg University
Aalborg
Denmark

Brady Wagoner
Department of Communication and Psychology
Aalborg University
Aalborg
Denmark

Aims of the Series

Both creativity and culture are areas that have experienced a rapid growth in interest in recent years. Moreover, there is a growing interest today in understanding creativity as a socio-cultural phenomenon and culture as a transformative, dynamic process. Creativity has traditionally been considered an exceptional quality that only a few people (truly) possess, a cognitive or personality trait 'residing' inside the mind of the creative individual. Conversely, culture has often been seen as 'outside' the person and described as a set of 'things' such as norms, beliefs, values, objects, and so on. The current literature shows a trend towards a different understanding, which recognises the psycho-socio-cultural nature of creative expression and the creative quality of appropriating and participating in culture. Our new, interdisciplinary series Palgrave Studies in Creativity and Culture intends to advance our knowledge of both creativity and cultural studies from the forefront of theory and research within the emerging cultural psychology of creativity, and the intersection between psychology, anthropology, sociology, education, business, and cultural studies. Palgrave Studies in Creativity and Culture is accepting proposals for monographs, Palgrave Pivots and edited collections that bring together creativity and culture. The series has a broader focus than simply the cultural approach to creativity, and is unified by a basic set of premises about creativity and cultural phenomena.

More information about this series at
http://www.springer.com/series/14640

Helen Owton

Doing Poetic Inquiry

palgrave
macmillan

Helen Owton
The Open University
Milton Keynes, UK

Palgrave Studies in Creativity and Culture
ISBN 978-3-319-64576-6 ISBN 978-3-319-64577-3 (eBook)
DOI 10.1007/978-3-319-64577-3

Library of Congress Control Number: 2017948282

Cover illustration: Pattern adapted from an Indian cotton print produced in the 19th century

Printed on acid-free paper

This Palgrave Macmillan imprint is published by Springer Nature
The registered company is Springer International Publishing AG
The registered company address is: Gewerbestrasse 11, 6330 Cham, Switzerland

To Ellie

Even if I don't always say—I'm really sorry,
For sometimes being a shabby mummy,
Sometimes I shout; noisy,
Get impatient; edgy,
I was like you sometimes,
probably,
Not listening; thinking it's funny,
Laughter chuckling in your tummy,
Jumping on the bed; hopping bunny,
Tumbling, dancing,
Not enough time just to play,
Sometimes I tell you off wrongly,
Cheeky monkey!
Other times you are just being naughty!
I try hide my worry,
Amidst the day to day hurry.
At the moment honey,
Things feel a bit cloudy
for me,
Past I was trying to bury,
Sometimes I get a bit stormy,

Not that you always see…
Working hard. Sorry,
If sometimes I'm too busy.
Sometimes, humming along together,
Tuned in endeavour,
Even if I don't always say,
I love you terribly…
How silly!
As if you didn't know that already!

Foreword

In a small, cramped office with flickering shade and light from a tree in the courtyard, Helen, the author of this volume, brings me to sudden tears. Sitting, with knees drawn up, she is reading out loud from one of her poems, after having completed the 'business' of our Ph.D. supervisory meeting. Other than following the death of my father, I have no memory of ever feeling slow tears slide down my cheek, whilst within one of the cool-rational spaces of academia, often construed as being so devoid of emotion. Helen's poem was about her grandfather and touched, gently, a nerve still unknowingly raw. I think perhaps I surprised her with my response to the words she spoke with such feeling. She looked taken aback. For me, in that flickering moment of intense intersubjectivity emerged a warm, emotional, shared understanding that I have never forgotten. This book offers readers pathways into such shared experience. It offers possibilities of stepping, however fleetingly, into another person's world to share some core elements of their experience. Helen uses Poetic Inquiry, often phenomenologically tinged, to encourage us as readers to step over the threshold and into someone else's lifeworld. And sometimes such border-stepping is painful, visceral-clutching. We encounter or half-sense uncomfortable recognition.

No prior familiarity with phenomenology, or with poetry and Poetic Inquiry are required, as the book explains and explores what a poem is, and why we might consider employing poetry as a form of research inquiry, and even as a form of self-care and therapy. The blending of poetry with other art forms such as drawing, photography, collage and video is also considered and explored, charting some of the rich possibilities generated by these creative linkages. As Helen notes, creative, artistic modes of expression can engender insights and findings that are not readily discovered via more conventional research approaches.

Ironically, crushing deadlines and work demands mean I have chance only to dip too briefly into this little tome, but fortunately, it is one of those books that invite happy dipping as well as longer and deeper immersion. Above (and beyond) all, this book is about poetry and the poetic, celebrating the possibilities, and also becoming aware of the (sometimes painful) challenges. Much has happened—to both of us—since that day in my poky, dusty office, but I still recall vividly my thoughts and feelings as Helen read to me her poem about her grandfather: A precious moment of insight, intersubjective touching and empathy.

Prof. Jacquelyn Allen-Collinson
University of Lincoln
Lincoln, UK

Acknowledgements

From my early years, I would like to thank my English teacher, Mr. Lewis, who introduced me to poetry at such a young age and to my English tutors at the University of Winchester who encouraged my curiosity.

There are a few academic friends I would like to thank; especially Emeritus Prof. Derek Jehu who has not only been a wonderful professional sounding board but an incredible friend with a great sense of humour—I feel very lucky to have met you and I don't think I would've found the confidence to write as much without you. I've built confidence from reading poems in public and academic related fields; I remember first reading my poems at a conference in 2011 where I was welcomed by a group of wonderfully supportive women at Cumberland Lodge who nurtured my feminist self. I am grateful to lots of academics striving to make a difference and encourage us to be, as quoted by Andrew Sparkes, 'unapologetic qualitative researchers'. In particular, I would like to thank Kitrina Douglas and David Carless who have paved the way towards an increasing acceptance of poetic wings of data. Both of you, along with Jacquelyn Allen-Collinson, are a constant source of inspiration, support and encouragement.

Thank you to my close friends, my family, my partner and my daughter for their ongoing encouragement, care, hugs and support; I feel surrounded by love and laughter. B, you light up my life. Also, I would like to thank Kathleen Curnock and her late husband, Bob, who have been like a family to me—your words of wisdom, compassion and laughs will haunt me forever.

Overview of Book

This book offers a phenomenologically inspired approach to sharing participants' stories in ways that paint pictures in the mind, allowing readers to walk inside the pictures and to step into someone else's world. Poetic Inquiry is one such way to allow readers this shared experience. In order to construct a poem, firstly, one needs to know what a poem is. Therefore, the book will start by explaining what poetry is, how poetry can appeal to our senses (e.g. imagery, hearing, touch, smell, taste) and the rationale for employing poetry as a research approach. Various different types of poetry can be employed and the four chapters that follow will focus on a few different types: poetry as data, turning data into poetry, poetry as literature review and poetry as reflective writing. According to some phenomenologists, we can know the world only through the senses; we must perceive first and reason second. Therefore, whilst taking a phenomenological approach (see Allen-Collinson 2009), Poetic Inquiry can be employed as a way of seeking to reveal something of the *essence* of people's key experiences. Additionally, the final two chapters consider how we might draw on characterising traits to judge Poetic Inquiry and how poetry might resonate with audiences so research can be disseminated more widely.

Key features:

- This book blends phenomenology with poetry.
- This book provides a detailed 'how to' guide to *doing* Poetic Inquiry.

- The book will explore different ways of employing poetry in research (e.g. poetry as data, turning data into poetry, poetry as literature review).
- Researchers can employ poetry as a self-care strategy and so this book will explore the possibility of poetry as therapy.
- Whilst there are some books on Poetry Inquiry and art as method, there is not a 'how to' guide to assist newcomers in research.

Contents

About the Author

Dr. Helen Owton is a Chartered Psychologist, Lecturer in Sport and Associate Lecturer in Psychology at the Open University, UK. Her research specialisms lie in innovative qualitative investigations (including arts-based methods) of sporting embodiment, sensory dimensions (e.g. audition, thermoception) and gendered sporting experiences covering topics that range from women's boxing, sportspeople with asthma and abuse in sport. She has written various books, book chapters and published in esteemed journals. She has been recognised for her innovative work by winning distinguished awards in her field of research.

List of Figures

List of Tables

CHAPTER 1

Introducing Poetic Inquiry

Abstract This section outlines the aims and summarises the chapters that follow and outlines what Poetic Inquiry entails. This section includes a brief literature review of what Poetic Inquiry is, how and why this is a useful methodology, what it can tell us that other methods can not and an overview of the chapters that follow.

Keywords Poetic inquiry · Arts-based methods · Qualitative methodology

My Footsteps into Poetic Inquiry

When I was 10 years old, Mr. Lewis had a profound impact on my English lessons when he introduced us to poetry. A few poems still linger in my memory, in my body, but one of my favourites was 'An Ordinary Day' by Norman MacCaig.

I took my mind a walk

Or my mind took me a walk –

Whichever was the truth of it.

H. Owton, *Doing Poetic Inquiry*, Palgrave Studies in Creativity and Culture, DOI 10.1007/978-3-319-64577-3_1

Reading this now, I can recognise the inquisitive and questioning nature of my younger self and why I might have been drawn to this art form. I wrote my first poem at the age of 10 years:

The Clear Blue Sea

I long to sail on a clear blue sea
Where the windy sky is blue,
"What shall we see today, my man,
Perhaps a shark or two."

We set out along the sea,
And past the nearest sailboard,
"Ahoy there, young fellowman"
And on the sail was a sword.

Suddenly, the wind blows up,
And the waves hurl inside
The swaying boat on the windy sea,
Nearly gets stuck in the tide.

The wind dies down,
And we're soaked to the bone
And I hear my partner say,
"I'm cold and tired
And I'm really hungry"
So we made our own way home.

Poetry has breezed in and out of my life at different times, and often it is associated with strong emotions. Even sceptics of poetry will, at some point in their lives, be drawn to poetry. Later, I was inspired after watching Dead Poets Society and struck by the late Robin Williams reciting John Keating's words 'No matter what anybody tells you, words and ideas can change the world'. As a mature student, I studied English for 2 years at university and used poetry to enter a different understanding about the death of my father.

On cloud Nine

The day he suddenly dropped dead
We float up one by one to the sky

Shocked into separation, nothing is said
We used to talk much, but now don't try

If he was here, he'd know what to say,
You weep and work, we say nothing, sleep, drift, stare...

The scholar'm us, she has to pay
It's not that you don't care

Not as good for floating in, this class
Each cloud more grey and complex, not right

At night we need coldness to pass
He's not here to wrap us up tight

Your life's shattered into smithereens
We obliviously float high above, that's our perk
Don't notice what's between's
Not thirty years or so, but work, work, work

[Inspired by Book Ends by Tony Harrison]

Eliot (1921) argues

> Poetry is not a turning loose of emotion, but an escape from emotion; it is not the expression of personality, but an escape from personality. But, of course, only those who have personality and emotions know what it means to want to escape from these things (Section II, pp. 36–39).

In August 2009, I began my Ph.D. journey and learned the excessive demands of balancing teaching and research; I felt the academic time-squeeze and I thought speed and efficiency were at the essence of my experience to demonstrate my competency in academic and scholarship fields. This made me critical about the value of busyness that our culture celebrates. As Berg and Seeber (2016, p. 55) argue, our perception of time and expectations of productivity need to be challenged and 'if we think of time only in terms of things accomplished ("done and done" as the new popular saying goes), we will never have enough of it'. These reflections led to me to question what, how, and why I do things in my professional practice and drew me back to poetry again. Pelias (2004) makes a plea for a *methodology of the heart* that is located in the researcher's body, 'a body deployed not as a narcissistic display but on behalf of others, a body that invites identification and empathetic connection, a body that takes as its charge to be fully human' (p. 1). The following poems attempt to show the process of this becoming; becoming a reflective poet-researcher:

Tough old boots

I used to love my tough old boots,
Conforming into the footprint moulds of preceding rough roots,
Sacrificing feet with bleeding pain,
Beaten into shape; endless relentlessness,
Ceaseless breathlessness,
Disciplinary conditioning plots needed to gain.

Dragged through dirtiest ditches, hoisted over soaring hills,
Sufferance of silent torn tread; emotional drainage,
Repetition in theory; emptiness kills,
Losing trodden meaning,
Yet controlled drama; stubborn defeatist; making me ill.

Exhausted weary hero tied to honour and glory,
My knotted body is a ruined temple!
A martyred journey to nowhere is a worry.

Difficulty heaving off these tough old boots,
May be needed, fending off bruits,
Perhaps ease them off—don't harm the interrelated roots.

Air the trapped stinking feet; let the poor wounds breathe,
Fresh footsteps absorb landscaping streams,
Energised by new twists and turns,
Stimulated by insightful themes,
Inscribing a way to ease the burns,
Discomfort easing; feet and well-being relieving.

[Inspired by The Field by Rose Flint]

Western society, particularly in academia, is typified somewhat by a 'disembodied' style of life (Leder 1990). A reaction against this trend towards corporeal engagement, against machines, computers and technologies, is to find ways of 'returning to the body' (Leder 1990). An attempt towards a 'decorporealised' existence can be via intimacy with nature (Leder 1990). With the shift in higher education towards more of an audit culture accompanied by a language of the machine, I made such an attempt to become more intimate with nature, and the images and language in the poem encouraged me to find a 'breathing space' for reflection and emotion, given the emotional labour involved in qualitative research (e.g. Hochschild 1983; Steinberg and Figart 1999; Brackenridge 1999) and family–work conflicting demands (see Canivet et al. 2010). Writing poetry enabled me to consider multiple possibilities in qualitative research.

Possibilities

Entrapment inside an institution crushing the souls of soldiers; a stranger.
An establishment hiding intentions; flaunting ambitions; a danger.

Release my body from embedded cultures that inhibit freedom to express personality.
Passivity; I see docile bodies consumed by habitual conformity,
"I don't have to think, I just have to do it!"

Uncomfortable tensions build; their desires to inflict control,
"Such enthusiastic camaraderie! *Just don't go overboard*"
Controlling people to fulfil their own ambitions; feeling sour.

Results are always fitting; awards, promotions; valiant tread,
Sensing hostility, rumours spread.

Fearless threatening suggestive touch; echoes of abusive power,
"*Only joking unless you were actually gonna do it!*"

Masked by the hidden codes of inflicting masculinity,
Tolerating the state of affairs in a situated freedom; a complex simplicity.
Knowing historical past; will we ever escape this tyranny?

Come on! Wake the fuck up!

Unfamiliar strangeness felt—leaning towards encouragement of risk and absurdity,
Desires for a world free from the limiting constraints of the past,
Passivity rejected; ever-risking the free play of just 'being' at last?
With a freedom to explore the world full of adventure,
Intertextual connections unfolding, opening the multiplicity of possibilities...

Often a life event or emotion encourages (or forces) people to write (Bolton 1999). During first year of my Ph.D., I wrote 35 poems which seemed to be the right time to write poetry for me. When life goes disastrously wrong, or wonderfully right, the emotions tend to be intense and the experience of events can feel jumbled (Becker 1999). Therefore, writing at this time may be cathartically useful—but it may not be possible to craft a poem (Bolton 1999). Indeed, poetry can create order out of mental turmoil or strife (Bolton 1999). An analysis of the poem gives a picture of the poet's heart. Poetry writing was found to be therapeutic during my doctoral study by relieving stress and frustration, releasing anger, promoting self-understanding and a 'filling in' of past memories. With acknowledgement of the role of the researcher as an instrument, much has been made of the need to be self-reflexive in analysing the 'baggage' of the researcher (Sparkes 1992). Consistent with Leder's (1990, p. 79) thoughts, I sought'whatever will help' in order 'to overcome the powerful urge to escape'.

Bridges of trust

Breakages of built bridges of trust,
Communities of learning,
Evaporating into dust.

Communities of competitiveness,
A paradox of hopes and ambitions,
Crumbling; a spark inside dies.

Returning to mistrust and withdrawnness,
Silence creeps back; not strong enough
For this crack
Of light.

Can't let it in.
If I don't seen the light,
I don't mind the darkness.

Question 'friendly' gestured motivation.
Better start with cynicism,
Than give trust freely; continuously broken.

I was happy
being unhappy.
Or was I just unhappy
being happy?

Like Leggo (2008), my poems are part of my ongoing engagement with living in the world and the poems are attempts to capture multiple moments, intensities and layers of struggle. Despite the risk of producing messy texts, Gilbourne (2010, 2011) emphasised the need for acceptance of these types of 'unsettling truths' because they can invoke new perspectives and invite fresh interpretations. Many argue that we need to continuously challenge the next emerging generation to step back from the 'status quo' of written conformity and to be prepared to critically review previous research instead of 'falling into line' as compliant scientific clones. Creative, artistic modes of expression can produce findings and insights not readily discoverable via more conventional research methods. Writing reflectively can highlight and bring these implicit awareness into a more explicit form which can then be analysed and reflected upon with fresh new eyes. As Butler-Kisber and Stewart (2009) argue, a poet can write from first-hand experience of the world, and in this sense *is* an empiricist; making observations of the world, where knowledge arises from evidence gathered via a sense experience. When I started my PhD, I felt frustrated with the limitations of criteria, external pressures and with what constituted 'good research'. Indeed, the words of Lemert (2002, p, 390):

> Stand on a street corner and look. You may see, but you may not understand. Sit on a corner and listen; you may hear but not quite understand. After a while, you might ask someone, "what the hell's goin' down here?" They may lie. They may tell you a story. Do this for a long while on as many corners as you can stand. Then you may be able to make poetry. Then, you may be able to make sociology. Then, you will be living a public life.

Whilst the three poems show a mixture of referenced intertextual connections, which would only be recognised or understood if certain texts have been read, Howard (2010) argues that our experiencing is always much more than recognising literary techniques and devices. After reflecting on historical paradigm battles of the past and the consequential fragmented impact of recent inflicting criteriology, I decided that I wanted to share my participants' stories in ways that painted pictures in the mind, allowing us to walk inside these pictures and to step into someone else's world (Sissay 2006). Additionally, silences provide space for thought which gaps in the poems allow for (Owton 2015a). I wanted to represent each person's stories in a way that also embraced the bond between us. Furman (2004) argues that 'the images inspired by a poem engage the reader in a creative relationship that moves beyond passivity to co-creation' (p. 163). Furthermore, Burns (2003) argues working viscerally and deeply means that readers may identify with the stories; they may learn from them or they may find them irrelevant. Working viscerally, Burns (2003) argues that we are more likely to be "drawn into it because something there speaks to our deeper selves, gets inside us and takes hold" (p. 1). Like Leggo (2008, p. 167), 'instead of living breathlessly, I am learning to live breath-fully'.

Like other forms of arts-based methods (e.g. vignettes, art), poetry invites the reader to 'step into' another person's experience. Furman (2004) argues that 'the images inspired by a poem engage the reader in a creative relationship that moves beyond passivity to co-creation' (p. 163). When poets use words that appeal to our senses (e.g., sight, hearing, touch, smell, taste, and balance, etc.), the poet 'shows' us rather than simply telling us and perhaps can transport us to a place, time, and experience, which, if the image is effective, allows us to understand the emotion being conveyed in the poem (Hogue 2006). Arts-based methods (a/r/tography), which evoke embodied responses in others, may also heighten the ways in which these felt-bodily states produce affective experiences in others, which is what I want to achieve (c.f. Richardson 2000). Poetic Inquiry is also a way to capture the nuances of any one person's experiences; often, listeners and readers tend to be moved by a poem's simplicity and power (Poindexter 2002). As Carol Ann Duffy says, 'I like to use simple words, but in a complicated way'. Furthermore, Machado (2016, p. 69) suggests we 'use emotionality as a tool to sharpen the reader's focus on what is affective, potent, and essential'.

Whilst poetry is a craft allowing us to experiment with language, rhythm and rhyme, Poetic Inquiry is a methodological approach that seeks to reveal and communicate multiple truths via intuitive contemplation and creative expression. Richardson (1997) opened the possibilities of experimental writing for others to follow. Now, there are a variety of different types of Poetic Inquiry that researchers engage in: research poetry (Poindexter 2002); data poetry (Commeyras and Montsi 2000); poetic representation (Richardson 1994, 1997); poetic narrative (Glesne 1997); anthropological poetry (Brady 2000); narrative poetry (Tedlock 1983; Owton 2015a, b, 2016a, b); poetic, fictional narrative (Smith 1999); ethno-poem (Smith 2002); map poems (Hurren 1998); fieldnote poems (Cahnmann 2003); investigative poetry (Hartnett 2003); interpretive poetry (Langer and Furman 2004); ethnographic poetics (Brady 2004; Denzin 1997); poetic social science (Bochner 2000); literature-voiced poetry (Prendergast 2006); tri-voiced poems (Leavy 2009, 2010); 'Vox Participare' (participant voiced poems) (Prendergast 2009). Leavy (2015) provides an even larger extensive list of different terms employed in Poetic Inquiry. These forms of expression emerged in response to theoretical developments (e.g. postmodern theory, postcolonial theory, feminist postmodernism, and feminist poststructuralism) which are concerned with articulating human experience by breaking down binaries, participant voices and relational power (Leavy 2015).

One might ask: *What qualifies you to conduct Poetic Inquiry?* Etherington (2004), amongst others, has highlighted the therapeutic aspects of poetry (see Chap. 6) and further suggests that we are all really poets. This may be so, nonetheless, researchers, such as Butler-Kisber and Stewart (2009) highlight such discussions about the professional practices of those who employ poetry as a tool of inquiry and urge them to read more poetry, take creative writing classes, and take more risks in our field notes and articles. As mentioned, my own experience in poetry stems from childhood exposure to poetry, poetry modules when studying English for 2 years at university, poetry readings and further attendances (and performances) at poetry evenings in the public and academic domain. I also publish poems with poetry publishers (Owton 2006, 2007, 2010, 2011, 2013a). I have published poetry in journals and book chapters (Owton 2012, 2013b 2015a, b, c, 2016a, b, c; Owton and Allen-Collinson 2016; Owton and Sparkes 2017). Whilst I might adhere to the idea that only those trained poetically and/or published researchers can justifiably undertake this type of research (Bishop and Willis 2014), I do not believe that poetry should be put on a pedestal.

Potentially, Poetic Inquiry is a 'revitalizing and galvanizing mode of thought for humanistic study and teaching, making available means of engaging with and producing texts that are both very fresh and steeped in poetic tradition' (Elliott 2012, p. iv). The power of poetic representation (if done well) lies in its ability to create evocative and open-ended connections to the data for the researcher, the reader and the listener (Rapport and Sparkes 2009). Poetic representation, specifically, is designed to stimulate and encourage multiple interpretations which invite and allow readers a greater interpretive freedom to make their own conclusions so that they are able better to understand this as they transfer this understanding into their own lives (Rapport and Sparkes 2009; Sparkes et al. 2003). Prendergast et al. (2009) reviewed the Poetic Inquiry as both a medium for representing data and for exploring lived experiences. Given this focus on lived experiences, taking a sociological-phenomenological approach (see Allen-Collinson 2009a), poetic representations can be employed as a way of seeking to reveal something of the *essence* of people's key experiences and as a window to view the complexities of understanding in a holistic way of knowing and being in the world. Additionally, Poetic Inquiry 'can join the creative with the researcher and allow them to work effectively together as catalyst for social action and change' (Edghill 2009, p. 298).

In this way, as previously noted, some would argue that poetry has the potential power to unite the poet and the reader/listener in the exact impulse or experience that led the poet to write the poem in the first place. Often, we find ourselves singing along to music perhaps because of the blend of rhythm, rhyme and melody that helps us remember it (Sinicki 2017); Duffy suggests that 'Poets sing our human music for us'. Perhaps, if poetry can tap into an individual's ability to 'do imagery' and this is critical to understanding, then perhaps this can be used as a starting point to help a person recall their own previous experiences, learn relaxation techniques, build confidence, and desensitise anxiety reactions to recover from anything distressing they might have experienced (Paivio 1985). Additionally, retaining and retrieving a memory might be much greater if the image touches deeper structures in the brain, operating both the verbal and image memory (see Paivio 1985 for detailed description of dual coding theory). Poetry could have the potential to prompt imagery by engaging the senses and consequently work with learn through experience to heighten self-understanding.

Overview of Chapters

The next chapter focuses on shaping Poetic Inquiry and explains how these arts-based methods might be epistemologically situated. The chapters that follow focus on different types of poetry that could be employed in the research context: Poetry as data; Poetry re-presentation; Poetry as literature review; Poetry as reflective writing. The last two chapters concentrate on how one might go about judging Poetic Inquiry and consider the future possibilities for Poetic Inquiry and other arts-based methods.

References

Allen-Collinson, J. (2009). Sporting embodiment sports studies and the (continuous) promise of phenomenology. *Qualitative Research in Sport and Exercise, 1*(3), 239–279.

Becker, G. (1999). *Disrupted lives: How people create meaning in a chaotic world.* Berkeley: University of California Press.

Berg, M., & Seeber, B. (2016). *Slow professor: Challenging the culture of speed in the academy.* Toronto: University of Toronto Press.

Bishop, E., & Willis, K. (2014). "Hope is that fiery feeling": Using poetry as data to explore the meanings of hope for young people. *Forum Qualitative Sozialforschung/Forum: Qualitative Social Research* (Vol. 15, No. 1). Available: http://www.qualitative-research.net/index.php/fqs/article/view/2013/3631. Accessed Apr 10, 2017.

Bochner, A. P. (2000). Criteria against ourselves. *Qualitative Inquiry, 6*(2), 266–272.

Bolton, G. (1999). 'Every poem breaks a silence that had to be overcome'*: The therapeutic power of poetry writing. *Feminist Review, 62,* 118–133.

Brackenridge, C. (1999). Managing myself: Investigator survival in sensitive research. *International Review for the Sociology of Sport, 34*(4), 399–410.

Brady, I. (2000). Three Jaguar/Mayan intertexts: Poetry and prose fiction. *Qualitative Inquiry, 6*(1), 58–64.

Brady, I. (2004). In defense of the sensual: Meaning construction in ethnography and poetics. *Qualitative Inquiry, 10*(4), 622–644.

Burns, M. (2003). Creative writing 101: Show vs. tell. *Colorado Springs Fiction Writer's Group.* Available: http://www.coloradospringsfictionwritersgroup.org/archive/2003-10_article-creative_writing_101-show_versus_tell.pdf. Accessed Nov 28, 2009.

Butler-Kisber, L., & Stewart, M. (2009). The use of poetry clusters in poetic inquiry. In M. Prendergast, C. Leggo, and P. Sameshima, P. (Eds.), *Poetic inquiry* (pp. 3–12). Boston: Sense. Rotterdam: Sense.

Cahnmann, M. (2003). The craft, practice, and possibility of poetry in educational research. *Educational Researcher, 32*(3), 29–36.
Canivet, C., Ostergren, P. O., Lindeberg, S. I., Choi, B., Karasek, R., Moghaddassi, M., and Isacsson, S. O. (2010). Conflict between the work and family domains and exhaustion among vocationally active men and women. *Social Science and Medicine, 70*(8), 1237–1245.
Commeyras, M., & Montsi, M. (2000). What if I woke up as the other sex? Batswana youth perspectives on gender. *Gender and Education, 12*(3), 327–346.
Denzin, N. (1997). Ethnographic poetics and narratives of the self. In N. Denzin, (Ed.). *Interpretative ethnography* (pp. 207–208). Thousand Oaks: Sage.
Edghill, G. (2009). The culture of my community revealed: Poetic and narrative beginnings. In M. Prendergast, C. Leggo & P. Sameshima (Eds.). *Poetic inquiry: Vibrant voices in the social sciences* (pp. 287–300). Rotterdam: Sense.
Eliot, T. S. (1921). T. S. Eliot (1888–1965). The Sacred Wood. Tradition and the individual talent. *Bartleby,* Available: http://www.bartleby.com/200/sw4.html. Accessed Oct 01, 2011.
Elliott, C. (2012). *Poetic inquiry.* Doctoral dissertation, University of Pittsburgh.
Etherington, K. (2004). *Becoming a reflexive researcher.* London: Jessica Kingsley.
Furman, R. (2004). Using poetry and narrative as qualitative data: Exploring a father's cancer through poetry. *Families, Systems, and Health, 22*(2), 162.
Gilbourne, D. (2010). The "edge of darkness" and "Just in Time": Two cautionary tales, two styles, one story. *Qualitative Inquiry, 16*(5), 325–331.
Gilbourne, D. (2011). 'Just in time': A reflective poetic monologue. *Reflective Practice, 12*(1), 27–33.
Glesne, C. (1997). That rare feeling: Re-presenting research through poetic transcription. *Qualitative Inquiry, 3*(2), 202–221.
Hartnett, S. J. (2003). *Incarceration nation: Investigative prison poems of hope and terror.* Lanham: Rowman Altamira.
Hochschild, A. R. (1983). *The managed heart.* Berkeley: University of California Press.
Hogue, D. (2006). What is a poem made of? Available: http://www.mshogue.com/poetry/made_of.html. Accessed Apr 11, 2011.
Howard, P. G. (2010). How literature works: Poetry and the phenomenology of reader response. *Phenomenology and Practice, 4*(1), 52–67.
Hurren, W. (1998). Living with/in the lines: Poetic possibilities for world writing.
Langer, C. L., & Furman, R. (2004, May). Exploring identity and assimilation: Research and interpretive poems. *Forum Qualitative Sozialforschung/Forum: Qualitative Social Research* (Vol. 5, No. 2).
Leavy, P. (2009). Fractured femininities/massacred masculinities: A poetic installation. *Qualitative Inquiry, 15*(9), 1439–1447.
Leavy, P. (2010). Poetic bodies: Female body image, sexual identity and arts-based research. *Learning Landscapes, 4*(1), 175–187.

Leavy, P. (2015). *Method meets art: Arts-based research practice*. New York: Guilford.

Leder, D. (1990). *The absent body*. Chicago: University of Chicago Press.

Leggo, C. (2008). Astonishing silence. In J. G. Knowles, & A. L. Cole (Eds.). *Handbook of the arts in qualitative research: Perspectives, methodologies, examples,and issues* (pp. 165–174).

Lemert, C. (2002). Poetry and public life. *Cultural Studies? Critical Methodologies, 2*(3), 371–393.

Machado, S. (2016). Faggot speaks: A poetic inquiry into the experiences of antigay mistreatment and sexual prejudice. *Art/Research International: A Transdisciplinary Journal, 1*(1), 65–87.

Owton, H. (2006). On cloud nine. In *Flight of fancy*. London: United Press.

Owton, H. (2007). Money, money, money. In *The thought that counts*. London: United Press.

Owton, H. (2010). Paper. In *Secrets of the heart*. London: United Press.

Owton, H. (2011). Unearthing the rug. *Diaries of united press*. London: United Press.

Owton, H. (2012). Streams of bereavement. *Qualitative Inquiry, XX*, 1–4.

Owton, H. (2013a). Smoking logic. In *Wings with words*. London: United Press.

Owton, H. (2013b). Integrating multiple forms of representation: Fighting asthma. *Qualitative Inquiry, 19*, 601–604.

Owton, H. (2015a). Performative embodiment and unravelling grandparent–grandchild Relationships. *Qualitative Inquiry, 21*(5), 426–435.

Owton, H. (2015b). A student–parent international experience. *Qualitative Methods in Psychology Bulletin, 20*, 15–17.

Owton, H. (2015c). Reinventing the body-self: Intense, gendered and heightened sensorial experiences of women's boxing embodiment. In A. Channon & C. Matthews (Eds.), *Global perspectives on women in combat sport: Women warriors around the world* (pp. 221–236). Basingstoke: Palgrave Macmillan. ISBN 978-1-137-43935-2.

Owton, H. (2016a). A father's son: I remember that day. *Qualitative Inquiry, 22*(7), 559–560.

Owton, H. (2016b). Tough old boots. *Psychology of Women's Section Review, 18*(1), 60.

Owton, H. (2016c). *A qualitative case study of sexual abuse in sport* (p. 109). Basingstoke: Palgrave. ISBN 978-3319467955.

Owton, H., & Allen-Collinson, J. (2016). 'It stays with you': Multiple representations of dance and future possibilities. *Qualitative Research in Sport, Exercise and Health, 9*(1), 49–55.

Owton, H., & Sparkes, A. (2017). Sexual abuse and the grooming process in sport: Bella's story. *Sport, Education and Society* (Online early). Available: http://www.tandfonline.com/doi/abs/10.1080/13573322.2015.1063484.

Paivio, A. (1985). Cognitive and motivational functions of imagery in human performance. *Canadian Journal of Applied Sport Sciences. Journal canadien des sciences appliquées au sport, 10*(4), 22S–28S.

Pelias, R. (2004). *A methodology of the heart: Evoking academic and daily life.* Walnut Creek, CA: AltaMira Press.

Poindexter, C. (2002). Research as poetry: A couple experiences HIV. *Qualitative Inquiry, 8,* 707–714.

Prendergast, M. (2006). Found poetry as literature review: Research poems on audience and performance. *Qualitative Inquiry, 12*(2), 369–388.

Prendergast, M. (2009). Introduction: The phenomena of poetry in research: "Poem is what?" Poetic inquiry in qualitative social science research. In *Poetic inquiry: Vibrant voices in the social sciences,* (pp. 13–29). Rotterdam: Sense Publishers.

Prendergast, M., Leggo, C., & Samashima, P. (Eds.). (2009). *Poetic inquiry: Vibrant voices in the social sciences.* Rotterdam, NL: Sense.

Rapport, F., & Sparkes, A. (2009). Narrating the Holocaust: In pursuit of poetic representations of health. *Journal of Medical Humanities, 35,* 27–34.

Richardson, L. (1994). Nine poems: Marriage and the family. *Journal of Contemporary Ethnography, 23*(1), 3–13.

Richardson, L. (1997). *Fields of play: Constructing an academic life.* New Brunswick: Rutgers University Press.

Richardson, L. (2000). Writing: A method of inquiry. In N. Denzin & Y. Lincoln (Eds.), *Handbook of qualitative research* (2nd ed., pp. 923–948). London: Sage.

Sinicki, A. (2017). Why do we remember songs so well? *Health Guidance.* Available: http://www.healthguidance.org/entry/17224/1/Why-Do-We-Remember-Songs-so-Well.html. Accessed Apr 25, 2017.

Sissay, L. (2006). *Reading poetry.* Available: http://www.poetrylibrary.org.uk/readinggroups/readingpoetry/. Accessed Apr 13, 2011.

Smith, P. (1999). Food truck's party hat. *Qualitative Inquiry, 5*(2), 244–261.

Smith, W. (2002). Ethno-poetry notes. *International Journal of Qualitative Studies in Education, 15*(4), 461–467.

Sparkes, A. (1992). *Research in physical education and sport: Exploring alternative visions.* London: The Falmer Press.

Sparkes, A., Nilges, L., Swan, P., & Dowling, F. (2003). Poetic representations in sport and physical education: Insider perspectives. *Sport, Education and Society, 8*(2), 153–177.

Steinberg, R. J., & Figart, D. M. (1999). Emotional labor since the managed heart. *The Annals of the American Academy of Political and Social Science, 561*(1), 8–26.

Tedlock, D. (1983). *The Spoken Word and the Work of Interpretation.* Philadelphia: University of Pennsylvania Press.

CHAPTER 2

Shaping Poetic Inquiry

Abstract This chapter focuses on positioning Poetic Inquiry philosophically with a discussion on paradigms. Also, I propose Poetic Inquiry can be shaped via meaningful methodologies specifically employing a phenomenologically inspired approach. This type of approach is well-placed as an approach to doing poetry with an emphasis on the mind-body-self nexus in relation to sensory experiences. Additionally, there is a focus upon the centrality of the 'visceral' body in the relationship between self-consciousness and the self. Details of this approach will set the scene for approaching various forms of Poetic Inquiry which are outlined later in the book.

Keywords Paradigms · Interpretivism · Phenomenology · Sensory experiences

Introduction

In order to understand Poetic Inquiry, it is important to position it in a discussion on *philosophical* foundations that are known as Paradigms. *Paradigms* are an overarching set of beliefs and provide orientations towards how researchers' assumptions perceive the world and how this view is used to break down the complexities of the 'real' world (Denzin and Lincoln 2000; Sparkes 1992). Markula and Silk (2011) argue that;

H. Owton, *Doing Poetic Inquiry*, Palgrave Studies in Creativity and Culture, DOI 10.1007/978-3-319-64577-3_2

> Paradigms are important because they provide the boundaries for the researcher's ethics and values, actions in the social world, the control of the study (who initiates the work, and asks questions), the voices deployed in the accounts of the research, and indeed, the very basic and fundamental understanding of the world the researcher is investigating (p. 25).

The positivistic paradigm is particularly prevalent in my specialised field—sport and exercise sciences—and it often serves to subordinate all other paradigms because of its assumed scientific authority. Often, positivists (e.g. experimental scientists) are hailed as the 'crowning achievements of Western civilization' (Denzin 2011, p. 2). *Positivism* is based on notions of an objective measurable reality, employing quantitative methods to predict and control research, with concepts of hypotheses, reliability, validity and objectivity (Sparkes 1992; Willig 2003). These methods within positivism are often taken to be the experts of truth, and knowledge is believed to rest on firm foundations that can be measured by scientific terminology or technical equipment (Denzin 2011; Sparkes 1992). Researchers working within this paradigm tend to view emotions as irrational, unscientific and/or contaminating of the research project (Tillmann-Healey and Keisinger 2001). Whilst positivists accuse the so-called new experimental qualitative researchers of writing fiction, not science with no way of verifying 'truth', Denzin (2011, p. 2) argues that 'there is little to be gained by attempting to engage in moral criticism' given the fixed and solid beliefs associated with positivism. In 'The Study of Poetry', Arnold (1880, Li 23–24) wrote that, 'Without poetry, our science will appear incomplete' and Wordsworth (cited in Arnold 1880, Li 27–28) calls poetry 'the impassioned expression which is in the countenance of all science'.

What can be learned from qualitative research is the importance of drawing upon and discussing one's own personal experiences and emotions during the research process, and those that are not, perhaps are being dishonest (Gilbert 2000). Arguably, the reader is not made aware as to the extent the researcher is conscious of her/his own biases and assumptions. Some argue that whilst paradigms are described and issues rehearsed being resolved 'in a bloodless, technical, and strangely old-fashioned counsel of perfection' the realities of qualitative research are much messier (Denzin 2011, p. 574). Traditional approaches have been extremely useful in social sciences, but Poetic Inquiry, where emotions are inextricably tied together, aims to capture the messiness of people's lives. When investigating the more complex, interchanging, subjective, emotional and individual lived experiences, the *interpretive* paradigm guides the way in which I approach and write up Poetic Inquiry. Before describing the interpretive paradigm, I detail how paradigms may be understood in terms of ***axiological, ontological, epistemological, rhetorical*** and ***methodological*** assumptions (Sparkes 1992).

Questions about ethics within the social world are known as axiological assumptions (Denzin and Lincoln 2011), and ontological assumptions concern the nature of the world, 'reality' and human beings in social contexts (Bryman 2001). One's epistemology is dependent upon beliefs and perceptions of truth; 'theory of knowledge' refers to the ways we acquire knowledge and what constitutes knowledge (Denzin and Lincoln 2011; Giacobbi et al. 2005). Methodological assumptions focus on providing a rationale for and analysing why we have selected methods used for attaining data (Sparkes 1992). According to Sparkes (1992), ontological assumptions give rise to epistemological assumptions which have methodological implications for data collection techniques, the way findings are interpreted and the ways they are written up in the final research project/papers. In this sense, paradigms guide all aspects of undertaking research (questions asked, ethical stances, actions, method choices, relationships to the participants, judgment of the quality of the research) (Markula and Silk 2011). Table 2.1 outlines some of the key paradigmatic frameworks that make up the world of research design.

Many qualitative researchers subscribe to a form of interpretivism (Smith and Sparkes 2016) which in many ways stands in opposition to the positivistic paradigm. Interpretivism has deeply embedded historical roots established in the nineteenth century, and contrary to positivism, the interpretative paradigm is underscored by very different ontological

Table 2.1 Based on Sparkes' (1992) Philosophical assumptions underlying the different paradigms (p. 21)

Assumptions	*Positivist*	*Interpretivist*	*Critical*
Ontology	External-realist	Internal-idealist, relativist	External-realist or internal-idealist
Epistemology	Objectivist-dualist	Subjectivist, interactive	Subjectivist, interactive
Methodology	Nomothetic, experimental, manipulative	Ideographic, heumeneutical, dialectical	Ideographic, participative, transformative
Interests	Prediction and control (technical)	Understanding and interpretation (practical)	Emancipation (criticism and liberation)

and epistemological assumptions, as Table 2.1 highlights (Sparkes 1992). Under the umbrella of the interpretative paradigm, approaches include ethnography, autoethnography, hermeneutics, naturalism, phenomenology, symbolic interactionism, constructivism, social constructivism, ethnomethodology, case study, essentially qualitative research (Sparkes 1992). Preissle (2011) employs different metaphors (tapestry, umbrella and bramble bush) to describe a variety of approaches. For example, she employs the metaphor of a *bramble bush* which encompasses fields of traditions and study that 'draw, borrow, or rob from one another in sometimes prickly fashion' (p. 689).

Poet-researchers do not aim to act in a distant, disembodied or dispassionate way (Gould and Nelson 2005; Leggo 2008). Instead, we acknowledge and integrate emotional experiences into our research (Tillmann-Healey and Keisinger 2001; Owton and Allen-Collinson 2014). In Poetic Inquiry, the poet-researcher's voice is always present in the research showing her/his role in the research process. The influence of the relationship between the researcher and participant is acknowledged in the production of data emerging from that interaction meaning that Poetic Inquiry cannot be reproduced exactly the same way. In this way, poet-researchers can act as a constructionist researcher, co-constructing knowledge, understanding and interpreting the meaning of lived experiences (Smith and Sparkes 2016). Furthermore, a critical researcher adopting Poetic Inquiry could involve 'being an activist and transformative intellectual' (Smith and Sparkes 2016, p. 3) where poetry is employed as a transformative tool.

Meaningful Approaches

Working from an interpretivist perspective, I believe that the meaning that individuals give to their experiences and their process of interpretation is essential, not accidental or secondary to the experience itself (Becker 1999). People interpret things from their past, from writings, families, TV, personalities, work and play (Becker 1999). It is in the interaction with these combined influences where an individual constructs meaning. Therefore, my aim is to work towards an understanding of the social milieu that is consistent with the experiences of the participants and to represent their accounts on a deep and meaningful level. I seek invitation into the intersubjective meanings (Gergen and Gergen 2002), that is of shared meanings, subjective states and processes of psychological energies moving between people.

I am also guided by feminist principles because I am concerned with 'issues of power, both societal power dynamics that impact and shape women's lives, as well as the power dynamics that exist between researcher and researched' (Cooky 2016, pp. 77–78). Whilst, 'giving voice' might be part of the outcome of Poetic Inquiry I tend to adopt a 'friendship as method' approach in an attempt to *get to know* others in meaningful and sustained ways (Fine 1994; Tillmann-Healy 2003; Owton and Allen-Collinson 2014; Castrodale and Zingaro 2015). Friendships, like fieldwork, have similar endeavours in that they both involve being in the world with others (Tillmann-Healy 2003). Friendship is described by Rawlins (1992) as an interpersonal bond characterised by the ongoing communicative management of dialectical tensions, such as those between idealisation and realisation, affection and instrumentality, and judgment and acceptance. This method encourages pathways towards actively undermining and disrupting the power imbalance between researcher and participant, reducing the hierarchical separation between them, which can be attempted through dialogue, relationships, and an ethic of caring that invites expressiveness, emotion and empathy (Tillmann-Healy 2003). It is unrealistic for a mutual, close and/or lasting friendship to develop between researcher and every participant, and so it is important not to unduly 'mislead' participants (Owton and Allen-Collinson 2014). Tillmann-Healy (2003) proposes that there is not necessarily a need to adopt the 'whole vision' to benefit from 'friendship as method', therefore I approach participants from a 'stance of friendship', meaning that I treat them with respect, honour their stories, and try to use their stories for humane and just purposes. With a particular focus on a feminist phenomenologically inspired approach, I bring ideas of existential phenomenology to the analysis of people's lived experiences and aim to sharpen the focus on corporeal embeddedness within cultural and social worlds (Allen-Collinson 2011a; Owton 2015a). As Allen-Collinson (2011a: 303) argues

> For feminist phenomenologists the 'personal' of phenomenology (first-person, subjective, experientially-grounded) is fundamentally linked to the 'political' (located within wider social, political and ideological structures).

Contrary to behaviourist approaches, symbolic interactionists, such as Mead (Silva 2007), claim that human interaction is mediated by social actors' interpretation of the situation, and/or the way each other's actions are defined (Silva 2007). Social actors do not simply react, but their 'response' is based on the meaning which they attach to such actions. The following ideas are central to this approach:

- The focus on the microscale social interactions between the actor, others and the world
- A view of both the actor and the world as dynamic processes and not static structures
- The actor's ability to interpret the social world.

Symbolic interactionism is a somewhat distinctive approach to the study of human group life and human conduct; it premises that human beings act towards things on the basis of the *meanings* that they have for them (Blumer 1969; Silva 2007). This emphasis on symbolism, signification, negotiated meaning and social construction of society, focuses attention on the roles people play (Silva 2007). This is not commonly explicitly recognised Poetic Inquiry. Goffman (1959) is a key advocate for studying roles dramaturgically by describing the way humans are role-playing actors following culturally formulated scripts; a theoretical perspective which provides one of the overarching frameworks for this research.

Identity is a common theme threaded through much poetry because many people write about what they know best. Poets often give us insight into their own worlds through their poetry which gives others a way to connect their own experiences, emotions and problems to better understand themselves. I draw upon symbolic interactionist-inspired conceptions (e.g. Goffman 1963, 1969) on identity. These conceptions emphasise the processual nature of self and identity (Allen-Collinson and Hockey 2007), where social actors and others engage in interactional work to actively develop and negotiate their selves in an intersubjective, dynamic and ongoing social process (Mead 1934). However, Shilling (1993) criticises Goffman for a failure to engage with the interactive dimensions of body management, and by assuming that categorisations of stigma can somehow exist prior to social encounters, although this perception is open to some debate. Some of Goffman's concepts might be a helpful to draw from.

Much of Goffman's work relates to the body and the ways in which people devise and maintain strategies for carrying out interactions with each other. Goffman (1959) argues that the presentation of self concerns the maintenance of a positive and convincing self-image. The body is the site where meaning is inscribed, which mediates the relationship between self-identity and social identity: consequently, the social meanings attached to the expression of bodily display are an extremely important factor in an individual's sense of self, and in his or her feelings of inner worth (Goffman 1959).

Goffman (1963), who was heavily influenced by the works of Mead, suggests that what matters in relation to a person's identity is not how the individual identifies her/himself but rather how others identify her/him. He also believed that all participants in social interactions are engaged in certain practices to avoid being embarrassed or embarrassing others (Goffman 1963) and thus to maintain the microsocial order. Goffman (1963) states that in some cases where a person could be stigmatised, it is possible for them to make an attempt to correct their condition by devoting much private effort (in the 'back regions' of one's life) to the mastery of areas of activity ordinarily felt to be closed on incidental and physical grounds to one with their 'shortcoming'. In order to prevent embarrassment and disruption to social interaction, Goffman (1963) refers to *impression management* and *dramaturgical discipline*. Goffman (1959) explains 'impression management' by employing the metaphor of 'dramaturgy', which permits a sociological understanding of the vital emotion of embarrassment. Embarrassment arises when the assumptions an interactant projects about her/his identity are threatened or discredited by the 'expressive facts' of the situation (Goffman 1967, pp. 107–108), which might lead to a 'spoiled identity'. For example, in Granny's poems (Owton 2015a), the poems demonstrate fluctuating interactions between the 'front regions' and 'back regions' of her life. In the 'back regions' of her theatre life, a considerable amount of dramaturgical discipline is invested in putting on a 'good face' for the 'front regions' of her life (Goffman 1959).

Phenomenologically Inspired Poetic Inquiry

A sociological phenomenological approach can *inspire* Poetic Inquiry by also exploring the interaction between mind-body-world. Like Poetic Inquiry, phenomenology is much more than a specific technique (Allen-Collinson 2016). According to some phenomenologists, we can know the world only through the senses; we must perceive first and reason second. Similarly to phenomenology, Poetic Inquiry is not a method, it is an attitude and a way of being and becoming in research and in the world. Leggo (2008, p. 168) explains;

> The poet-researcher seeks to live attentively in the moment, to seek to enter lived experiences with a creative openness to people and experiences and understandings.

Through this phenomenologically inspired approach, I subscribe to the phenomenological quest to, 'attempt to suspend our "adult" knowledge and preconceptions in order to view the world through the fresh, excited, "naive" eyes of childhood' (Allen-Collinson 2011b, p. 4). This approach aligns with poetry since it 'is not based upon linear cause and effect logic; a poem does not need to "make sense"' (Furman 2007, p. 2). Allen-Collinson (2016) aligns herself with Varela (1996) and Ravn and Christensen (2014) who call for phenomenology to be 'a specific type of reflection or attitude about our human capacity for, and mode of, being conscious' (p. 15). Merleau-Ponty (2002), a leading existentialist and phenomenological writer, describes reflection as not withdrawing from the world's basis:

> it steps back to watch the forms of transcendence fly up like sparks from a fire; it slackens the intentional threads which attach us to the world and thus brings them to our notice; it alone is consciousness of the world because it reveals that world as strange and paradoxical (p. xv).

Phenomenology offers a strong theoretical tradition, which also highlights the crucial role that the *senses* play in our experiences (Hockey and Allen-Collinson 2007; Allen-Collinson and Hockey 2007, 2009, 2010; Sparkes 2009). Phenomenologically speaking, being aware of the senses in poetry both when writing, when writing about and when listening to, is central. There has been an over portrayal of the visual in much of the research on senses therefore other sensory dimensions have been neglected, yet Sparkes (2009) stresses not to 'advocate replacing one sensory bias with another' as part of an 'anti-visualist agenda' (p. 31). As Paterson (2011, para 6) argues 'we never perceive by vision alone', and he further questions how haptic or 'more-than visual' knowledges are conceptualised and operationalised. For example, Paterson (2011, para 6) argues that:

> We have many expressions about 'knowing' that invoke touch, such as wanting a 'hands on' experience. Especially in our relation to 'things', we desire to know them through closeness and the mediation of our touch.

These bodily (somatic) senses inform our perception of 'inside' and 'outside', of inner and outer space (Paterson 2009). In phenomenology, this neat distinction between inside and outside or interior and exterior is problematized (Merleau-Ponty 1969) and 'rather than discrete and separate, these senses act in concert to help give us our embodied perceptions of space' (Paterson 2009, p. 768). Forms of corporeal knowledge or 'carnal knowing' are connected deeply to sensory experience (Mellor and Shilling 1997, p. 56). This seems to be well aligned with Poetic Inquiry given the messiness this type of inquiry allows (Krane 2016). Commensurate with the phenomenological approach, when poets use words that appeal to our senses (e.g. sight, hearing, touch, smell, taste and balance) the poet 'shows' us rather than simply telling us and perhaps can transport us to place, time and experience. Therefore, how we might 'return to our senses' is particularly important in connection with the phenomenological idea of self-understanding (Block and Block 2005).

The phenomenological view believes that our body is always in relationship to itself, with others, with human space and time, and everything affects it in terms of how we experience ourselves and the world around us (Allen-Collinson 2009a). Consciousness is always consciousness of something and therefore intentional which means it is always directed towards something (Leder 2001; Merleau-Ponty 2001). Phenomenologists, such as Merleau-Ponty 2001) believe that 'to begin with the lived body is to understand the physiological as always intertwined with, and an expression of, the body's *intentionality*[1]' (Owton 2015b, p. 224). As such, according to phenomenologists, people's experiences should be understood in the context of the person's *existential* grasp of the world (Leder 2001; Merleau-Ponty 1962). Similarly, symbolic interactionists believe that consciousness is not separated from action and interaction; it is an integral part of both (Silva 2007). Leder (1992) argues that taking a phenomenological approach offers the possibility of a 'sensitive analysis of the relationship between the self, identity and the body' (cited in Nettleton 1995, p. 108). Given that poets often tell us quite a bit about themselves in poems, the specific ways we experience ourselves as embodied thus become prime data for theorising about knowledge and experience.

In this sense, therefore, Poetic Inquiry can explore how people might act towards things associated in their lifeworld and these meanings that things have for humans are central in their own right (Blumer 1969).

Theoretical perspectives that focus upon the importance of meaning making in everyday life can be employed in Poetic Inquiry in order to offer an insight not only into the individual's meaningful experience and embodiment but also into the ways in which people share their embodied experiences in various environments. Whilst I adhere to a feminist phenomenologically inspired approach to Poetic Inquiry, as Denzin (2010) reminds us, it is important to remember that there is no one way to do interpretive qualitative inquiry. He argues;

> We are all interpretive bricoleurs stuck in the present working against the past as we move into a politically charged and challenging future (Denzin 2010, p. 15)

Bricoleurs, in this sense, are interpreters working to construct or create research from a diverse range of methodological tools available to us and the process in which such work is created.

Performativity

A shift towards a willingness to experiment with alternative new representational forms has been accompanied by the move to performance (Denzin 2010). Denzin (2010) argues for a performance studies paradigm: one, which 'understands performance simultaneously as a form of inquiry and as a form of activism, as critique, as critical citizenship' (p. 18). Denzin (2001) argues that we inhabit a performance-based, dramaturgical culture where the dividing line between performer and audience blurs, and culture itself becomes a dramatic performance. 'Performance is a way of knowing, a way of creating and fostering understanding, a method that persons use to create and give meaning to everyday life' (Denzin 2010, p. 30). As argued earlier, engaging participants as a poet-researcher is not a top-down process of gathering data, but a reciprocal relationship in which insights are developed and shared. Given this, poetry and other arts-based methods can be appropriate and particularly powerful tools for achieving these aims. When I read poems to an audience, I am making my performative role explicit.

Many researchers acknowledge and understand how the interview itself is a performance in which each performer (or social actor) actively selects how they will respond to each other (Denzin 2001; Ezzy 2010). This understanding has grown out of symbolic interactionist traditions including via Denzin's (2001) appreciation of Goffman's work that argues that we inhabit a performance-based, dramaturgical culture where the dividing line between performer and audience blurs, and culture itself becomes a dramatic performance. Therefore, to listen effectively involves *seeing* as well as *hearing* that person. More importantly, this also involves being aware of one's own non-verbal messages (gesture, body-posture, eye contact, tone, facial expression), which is an important part of communication. When performing poems from transcribed interview verbatim, these nuanced expressions might be captured more visibly when performing poems to audiences.

Whilst I recognise my performative role in research, I recognise the limitations of 'page' poetry identified by Wade (2011, p. 13) which include:

- Linked with serious philosophy
- Written with the use of private reference
- Presented elaborate syntax
- Used obscure vocabulary and imagery.

'Page' poetry, however, is actually a relatively new idea in poetry. Historically, poetry has been written with performance in mind since c.1000 A.D. when the Anglo-Saxon epic *Beowulf* was read aloud to an audience and medieval times when poets performed their poetry to music (Wade 2011). The 1960s pushed for a shift back to performativity in a quest for a more flexible approach which touches on ongoing debates about issues of representation, which often appears to be about the prioritising and valuing the *written* word over *verbal* and *visual* word (Richardson 1997). By offering this guide, it is not meant to devalue the importance of either type of representation, but it is aimed at seeing how to start developing and nurturing your reflective, poetic, performative self (Douglas and Carless 2008) in ways that offer new ways of 'knowing' and 'seeing'.

Note

1. Merleau-Ponty (2001) focuses on bodily intentionality—the body as an attitude directed towards an existing or potential task. For him, intentionality, perception and action are fundamentally intertwined. See Allen-Collinson (2011a, b) for examples of Merleau-Ponty's existential approach and the concept of intentionality.

References

Allen-Collinson, J. (2009). Sporting embodiment sports studies and the (continuous) promise of phenomenology. *Qualitative Research in Sport and Exercise, 1*(3), 239–279.

Allen-Collinson, J. (2011a). Feminist phenomenology and the woman in the running body. *Sport, Ethics and Philosophy, 5*(3), 297–313.

Allen-Collinson, J. (2011b). Intention and epoche in tension: Autophenomenography, bracketing and a novel approach to researching sporting embodiment. *Qualitative Research in Sport and Exercise, 3*(1), 48–62.

Allen-Collinson, J. (2016). Breathing in life: Phenomenological perspectives on sport and exercise. In B. Smith & A. Sparkes (Eds.). *Routledge Handbook of Qualitative Research in Sport and Exercise* (pp. 11–23). London: Taylor & Francis Ltd.

Allen-Collinson, J., & Hockey, J. (2007). 'Working out' identity: Distance runners and the management of disrupted identity. *Leisure Studies, 26*(4), 381–398.

Allen-Collinson, J., & Hockey, J. (2009). The essence of sporting embodiment: Phenomenological analyses of the sporting body. *The International Journal of Interdisciplinary Social Sciences, 4*(4), 71–81.

Allen-Collinson, J., & Hockey, J. (2010). Feeling the way: Notes towards a haptic phenomenology of distance running and scuba diving. *International Review for the Sociology of Sport, 46*(3), 1–16.

Arnold, M. (1880). The study of poetry. Available: https://www.academia.edu/25832840/Arnold_Study_of_Poetry. Accessed 25 Apr 2017.

Becker, G. (1999). *Disrupted lives: How people create meaning in a chaotic world.* Berkeley: University of California Press.

Block, S., & Block, C. (2005). *Come to your senses: Demystifying the mind-body connection.* Oregon: Beyond Words Publishing.

Blumer, H. (1969). *Symbolic interactionism: Perspective and method.* Englewood Cliffs, NJ: Prentice-Hall.

Bryman, A. (2001). *Social research methods.* Oxford: Oxford University Press.

Castrodale, M. A., & Zingaro, D. (2015). "You're such a good friend": A woven autoethnographic narrative discussion of disability and friendship in Higher Education. *Education, 35*, 1.

Cooky, C. (2016). *Feminisms.* In B. Smith & A. Sparkes (Eds.). *Routledge handbook of qualitative research in sport and exercise* (pp. 75–87). London: Routledge.

Denzin, N. K., & Lincoln, Y. (2000). *Qualitative research.* Thousand Oaks ua, 413–427.

Denzin, N. (2001). The reflexive interview and a perfomative social science. *Qualitative Research, 1*(1), 23–46.

Denzin, N. (2010). *The Qualitative Manifesto: A call to arms*. Walnut Creek, CA: Left Coast Press.

Denzin, N. K., & Lincoln, Y. S. (2011). *The Sage handbook of qualitative research*. Thousand Oaks: Sage.

Denzin, N. K. (2011). *The politics of evidence*. The Sage handbook of qualitative research, 645–657.

Douglas, K., & Carless, D. (2008). Nurturing a performative self. *Forum: Qualitative Social Research, 9*(2), Art. 23.

Ezzy, D. (2010). Qualitative interviewing as an embodied emotional performance. *Qualitative Inquiry, 16*(3), 163–170.

Fine, M. (1994). Working the hyphens: Reinventing self and other in qualitative research. In N. Denzin & Y. Lincoln (Eds.). *Handbook of qualitative research* (pp. 70–82). London: Sage.

Furman, R. (2007). Poetry and narrative as qualitative data: Explorations into existential theory. *Indo-Pacific Journal of Phenomenology, 7*(1), 1–9.

Gergen, M., & Gergen, K. J. (2002). Ethnographic representation as relationship. In A. Bochner & C. Ellis (Eds.). *Ethnographically speaking* (pp. 11–33). Walnut Creek: AltaMira Press.

Gilbert, K. (Ed.). (2000). *The emotional nature of qualitative research*. Boca Raton: CRC Press.

Giacobbi, P., Poczwardowski, A., & Hager, P. (2005). A pragmatic research philosophy for sport and exercise psychology. *The Sport Psychologist, 19*, 18–31.

Goffman, E. (1959). *The presentation of self in everyday life*. London: Penguin Books.

Goffman, E. (1963). *Stigma: Notes on the management of spoiled identity*. Englewood Cliffs, NJ: Prentice Hall.

Goffman, E. (1967). *On face-work*. Interaction ritual, 5–45.

Goffman, E. (1969). *Strategic interaction*. Philadelphia: University of Pennsylvania Press.

Gould, J., & Nelson, J. (2005). Researchers reflect from the cancer precipice. *Reflective Practice, 6*(2), 277–284.

Hockey, J., & Allen-Collinson, J. (2007). Grasping the phenomenology of sporting bodies. *International Review for the Sociology of Sport, 42*, 115–131.

Krane, V. (2016). Embracing the messiness of qualitative research: Challenges and opportunities for qualitative researchers in sport and exercise. In B. Smith & A. C. Sparkes (Eds.). *Routledge handbook of qualitative research in sport and exercise*. London: Routledge.

Leder, D. (1992). A tale of two bodies: The Cartesian corpse and the lived body. In *The body in medical thought and practice* (pp. 17–35). Springer Netherlands.

Leder, D. (2001). Lived Body: A tale of two bodies: The Cartesian corpse and the lived body. In D. Welton (Ed.). *Body and flesh: A philosophical reader* (pp. 117–129). Oxford: Blackwell.

Leggo, C. (2008). Astonishing silence. In G. Knowles & A. Cole (Eds.). *Handbook of the arts in qualitative research* (pp. 165–174). Thousand Oaks, CA: Sage.

Markula, P., & Silk, M. (2011). *Qualitative research for physical culture: Design, data collection and dissemination.* Basingstoke: Palgrave Macmillan.

Mead, G. (1934). *Mind, self, and society.* Chicago: University of Chicago Press.

Mellor, P. A., & Shilling, C. (1997). *Re-forming the body: Religion, community and modernity* (Vol. 50). London: Sage.

Merleau-Ponty, M. (1962). *Phenomenology of perception.* London: Routledge.

Merleau-Ponty, M. (1969). *The visible and the invisible: Studies in phenomenology and existential philosophy.* Trans. by Alphonso Lingis. Chicago: Northwestern University Press.

Merleau-Ponty, M. (2001). Psychologie et pédagogie de l'enfant.: Cours de Sorbonne, 1949–1952. Editions Verdier.

Merleau-Ponty, M. (2002). *Phenomenology of perception.* Trans. by Colin Smith. London: Routledge.

Nettleton, S. (1995). *The sociology of health and illness.* Cambridge: Polity Press.

Owton, H. (2015a). A student-parent international experience. *Qualitative Methods in Psychology Bulletin, 20,* 15–17.

Owton, H. (2015b). Reinventing the body-self: Intense, gendered and heightened sensorial experiences of women's boxing embodiment. In A. Channon & C. Matthews (Eds.). *Global perspectives on women in combat sport: Women warriors around the world* (pp. 221–236). Basingstoke: Palgrave Macmillan. IBSN 978-1-137-43935-2.

Owton, H., & Allen-Collinson, J. (2014). Close but not too close: Friendship as method(ology) in ethnographic research encounters. *Journal of Contemporary Ethnography, 43*(3), 283–305.

Paterson, M. (2009). Haptic geographies: ethnography, haptic knowledges and sensuous dispositions. *Progress in Human Geography, 33*(6), 766–788.

Paterson, M. (2011). Haptics. *Senses of Touch.* Available: http://geotheory.wordpress.com/space/. Accessed 20 May 2011.

Preissle, J. (2011). Qualitative futures: Where we might go from where we've been. In N. K. Denzin & Y. S. Lincoln (Eds.). *The SAGE handbook of qualitative research* (4th ed., pp. 685–698). Los Angeles: SAGE.

Ravn, S., & Christensen, M. K. (2014). Listening to the body? How phenomenological insights can be used to explore a golfer's experience of the physicality of her body. *Qualitative Research in Sport, Exercise and Health, 6*(4), 462–477.

Rawlins, W. K. (1992). *Friendship matters: Communication, dialectics, and the life course.* London: Transaction Publishers.

Richardson, L. (1997). *Fields of play: Constructing an academic life. New.* Brunswick: Rutgers University Press.

Shilling, C. (1993). *The body and social theory*. London: Sage.
Silva, F. (2007). *G.H. Mead: A critical introduction*. Cambridge: Polity Press.
Smith, B., & Sparkes, A. C. (2016). Qualitative interviewing in the sport and exercise sciences. In B. Smith & A. C. Sparkes (Eds.). *Routledge handbook of qualitative research in sport and exercise*. London: Taylor & Francis Ltd.
Sparkes, A. (1992). *Research in physical education and sport: Exploring alternative visions*. London: The Falmer Press.
Sparkes, A. (2009). Ethnography and the senses: Challenges and possibilities. *Qualitative research in sport and exercise, 1*, 21–35.
Tillmann-Healy, L. (2003). Friendship as Method. *Qualitative Inquiry, 9*(5), 729–749.
Tillmann-Healey, L., & Keisinger, C. (2001). Mirrors: seeing each other and ourselves through fieldwork. In K. Gilbert (Ed.). *The emotional nature of qualitative research* (pp. 81–110). Florida: CRC Press.
Varela, F. J. (1996). Neurophenomenology: A methodological remedy for the hard problem. *Journal of Consciousness Studies, 3*(4), 330–349.
Wade, S. (2011). *A straightforward guide to writing performance poetry*. Brighton: Straightforward Publishing.
Willig, C. (2003). *Introducing qualitative research in psychology: Adventures in theory and method*. McGraw Hill Education: Open University Press.

CHAPTER 3

Poetry as Data

Abstract This section outlines how poetry can be employed and analysed. At times, participants might provide a poem to the researcher as a way to help others understand their experiences. Whilst there are many examples of poetry, there are not many examples of poetry as data and the different ways this could manifest itself in Poetic Inquiry. I draw from research which considers how poetry could be a way to engage participants about a particular research topic. Examples are employed from poetry which have been provided by participants in my research. More commonly, it seems, poetry as data has been employed by researchers as auto-ethno poetry which is discussed towards the end of this chapter with examples from research I have conducted in women's boxing.

Keywords Poetry as data · Collaborative autoethnography poetry Auto/ethno poetry · Ethics

Poetry as Data

In the arts, it is typical to study poems (poetology—the study of verse) and explore meanings, a poet's identity, society, rhythm, rhyme, metaphors, imagery and structure. Yet poetry as data appears to be an approach missing in arts-based methods. Whilst poet-researchers might employ an autoethnograpic approach to using poetry as data and subject their own poetry to analysis (e.g. Machado 2016), there are a limited

H. Owton, *Doing Poetic Inquiry*, Palgrave Studies in Creativity and Culture, DOI 10.1007/978-3-319-64577-3_3

number of studies employing poetry written by participants. The high-brow nature of poetry seems to have seeped into the arts-based methods circle where there are ongoing debates about inferiority, superiority, poetry as data or art, and what qualifies one to write and publish poetry (Piirto 2002; Prendergast 2009; Shapiro 2004). Some argue whether Poetic Inquiry is '*art* or merely '*art-like*' (Prendergast 2009, p.xxv) with an *art* versus *data* debate emerging. 'There is something vaguely jarring about the juxtaposition of these two words. Finding them together in the same sentence may seem bold to some, oxymoronic to others, or perhaps even just moronic' (Shapiro 2004, p. 172). Bishop and Willis (2014, para 4.1) view poetry as art *and* data and point out that other forms of 'qualitative data are manifold, including completed sentences, traditional sculpture, body sculpture, and even finger painting. Suffice to say, participants' poetry can also be classified and analysed in this way.'

Nonetheless, these debates could point towards why poetry is less likely to be employed as data from participants. The difficulty with so few examples is that we lack the learning experiences from these projects on how to improve this practice. There are some examples, however, we can draw from which includes some of my own research. Firstly, Bishop and Willis (2014) decided to employ poetry to engage young people and produce data about the concept of hope that reflected their experiences. Given the uncommon practice of asking participants to write poetry, they drew from Eckersley et al. (2007) research employing workshop activities and drama techniques with young people to explore their perceptions of the future. In turn, they asked participants to write a poem or a story about hope by presenting a number of different poetic styles and alternatives. Given the pedestal poetry is often positioned on, they recognised the difficulty, some participants might have in writing a free verse poem in a short period of time. Therefore, they made an effort to explain to students that they were not looking for crafted 'works of art' and emphasised their belief that poetry is not necessarily highbrow or complex but they believe that poetry can offer a window into their everyday experiences. Furthermore, they gave their participants options of either writing a freestyle poem or using a formal poetry structure. The options are listed below, but the majority of the participants selected either Acrostic or a 'Sense' poem:

Acrostic poem:	the first letter of each line spells out a word vertically. For the purpose of this project they used the letters H.O.P.E.

Sense poem: they complete different phrases focused on the senses:

Hope tastes like…,
Hope sounds like…,
Hope smells like…,
Hope looks like…,
Hope makes me feel…,

Free verse poem: these poems provided freedom for participants to write how they
wished. There is no structure, no set rhythm of the words (meter), and
no rhyming scheme.

From their engagement with the data and discussion of findings, Bishop and Willis (2014, para 5.1) noted the following points:

1. The simple acrostic structure provided students with a stimulus in the form of the letters H-O-P-E, and responses are necessarily restricted to these stimulus letters.
2. The sense poems also encouraged participants to tap into the affective dimensions of hope.
3. The participants who utilised the free verse approach often spent more time on the activity. This might indicate a closer engagement with, and deeper consideration of, the concept under scrutiny. Perhaps these poems therefore provide greater insight into the lived experience of the author. Regardless, they were characterised by a greater use of imagery and a more complex syntax and structure which produced more nuanced and less consistently positive themes than the acrostic and sense poems.

Bishop and Willis (2014) make a point of including examples of the participants' poems to uphold their promise to participants as well as let the reader make their own interpretations of the full data available. As well as employing these poems to discuss understandings of the meanings young people attribute to hope, they draw from the process of this type of Poetic Inquiry and add to the debate on *art* versus *data*. They note that whilst the young people's poems might not be considered 'good poems in and of themselves' (Prendergast 2009, p. 545), they found that poems had been thoughtfully constructed and offered beautiful imagery and powerful language, providing data that is 'highly consumable and emotionally evocative' (Furman et al. 2007, p. 304). Furthermore, they argue that on the merits of poetry research, '[w]hile poetry may not commonly be thought of as a source of knowledge, poems are powerful documents that possess the capacity to capture the contextual and psychological worlds of both poet and subject' (Furman et al. 2007, p. 302). In this sense, Poetic Inquiry allows a similar type of analysis to other traditional types of qualitative research. Poetry as data permits participants to write poetry in response to various research topics, which can be subjected to analysis in a similar way to other traditional types of qualitative data (Bishop and Willis 2014).

Poetry as data has been employed in medical professions. For example, Shapiro and Stein (2005) examined, poetry written by medical students to explore the students' relationships with patients, patients' families and supervisors. Similarly, Henderson (2002) examined three medical student poems about death. These were analysed by exploring various elements of poetry, such as emotional expression, thoughts, vivid detail and metaphor.

Collaborative Autoethnography Poetry

As qualitative researchers, we recognise that sometimes research takes unpredictable turns which can often be a wonderful stroke of luck. During a case study research project on sexual abuse in sport, 'Bella' produced a large number of vignettes and poems that she felt best described her experiences of sexual abuse in sport. With her permission, selected vignettes and poems were published in a book (Owton 2016) and in an articles (Owton and Sparkes 2017; Owton and Allen-Collinson 2017). Given this combined approach, I engaged in a process called *collaborative autoethnography* via friendship as method approach which involved engaging in acute and sustained reflexivity and self-scrutiny (Owton 2016). Collaborative autoethnography can vary according to different models of collaboration (Ngunjiri et al. 2010), but for the purpose of this project, it involved producing an evocative performance text with the co-writer/participant. Similarly to Allen-Collinson and Hockey (2001), and given the highly sensitive nature of the topic, any identifying features were eliminated if they were deemed to expose the anonymity of those involved. Aside from these edits, Bella's poems were untouched and left to speak for themselves. Whilst I offered some reference to relevant theories in the book, I wanted the reader to act as 'interpretive listener' and apply their own theories and experiences to what they read/heard. What follows, are three examples of poetry written by Bella about her experiences of sexual abuse in sport. At this juncture, I would like to emphasise the potentially distressing nature of these poems and again, I ask readers to act as interpretive listeners.

Introducing Bella Aged 13

A weak skinny runt,
Building confidence; self-esteem,
Training techniques, hard graft; rough regime,
Enhanced bodily control; bear the brunt.

Years of dedication; tough girl built,
Perfected sequenced flowing moves,
Performances never wilt,
Masculinity she had to prove.

Look closer…
Take off the concealed cloak,
Behind this loyal dutiful kid,
Accumulative little sordid secrets hid…

My coach

My coach, respected,
Feared rejected,
Father figure allocated.

First time, 14,
Round his house,
Slowly building on trust; dependency,
Attention; days were funny.

Teased; humiliation always on the brink,
Naughty treats; competitions, let us drink,
Worked for him,
Massaged him…

One day, *"Your turn!"* laying on his sofa, slowly,
"Your bra's in the way,"
Irritation,
Sliding up top, sliding down trousers,
Fingers sliding up legs, slipping up inside, too much attention!

Remembering horrible feeling,
Wrong, wrong, wrong,
Frozen in shame,
Him worrying too; feeling the same.

Wanting so badly to be loved,
Feared of being rejected;
Pushed out the elite squad, club,
Compliance; ultimately accepted.

Loyalty tested,
Our little secret.

A lucky escape

I fell for your stealth,
For too long, finally leaving,
Staying I would have failed myself!

Now, *slowly* path
Re-learning from the past,
I think I've probably had the worst!

A new life; a bodily pulsating process
Through which I awake,
No shame; *your* shame,
Thank goodness I had a lucky escape.

Ethical Considerations

Working with Bella required a lot of time and patience; given the sensitive nature of the topic. Ethically, it was important to ensure that Bella was ready (more than ready) to publish her work. Whilst Bella found this process therapeutic and wanted to help others by sharing her story and help shape policy and practice in all sports (Owton 2016; Owton and Allen-Collinson 2017; Owton and Sparkes 2017), there was also a risk of her experiencing a 'double trauma' (Owton 2016; Owton and Allen-Collinson 2017; Owton and Sparkes 2017). Given that Bella was a vulnerable participant, she engaged in other therapy work to discuss the writing process in a safe space and navigate when she was ready to disclose this to the public. This process took years, and it was only when we really felt that she was ready to release her work into the public after discussions around ownership that her work was published (Owton and Sparkes 2017). It is important to consider these ethical concerns when using poetry as data because once people have listened to poems (and stories), they cannot be unheard (King 2003).

Auto/Ethno Poetry

Like others (e.g. Drummond 2017; Furman 2006; Blinne 2010; Maurino 2016), I have drawn on Poetic Inquiry (and narrative) to write autoethnographically about various research topics (e.g. boxing). This can be referred to as autoethno poetry.

It's good to be back

Another year gone, gone quick
Days filled with routine,
Squeezing in training,
Round busy days filled with working,
Studying, writing,
Parenting,
Oh! And trying
To get some sleeping!

Arriving here again,
Soaking up the sun, I feel relief,
Breathing easy, washing away grief,
In myself, feelings of healthy belief,
again.
This year… starting combat, reclaiming my fighting roots,
Never thought I'd put back on my brave boots,
Bouncin, punchin, kickin,
again.

Pads hitting – bobbing 'n' weaving, arms aaaaachin,
Shuttles, squats, jumping lunges - legs screeaamin,
Panting, sweating, chest buuuuurstin,
Enjoying feelings
Of fuckin working,
Time to enjoy my body - tough training,
Maintain! Keep pushin,
Ahhhhh,
it's good to be back!

It'll be good to be back
again.

I could do that!

The Olympic final, women's boxing,
Nicola Adams fighting,
"Is this men's or women's?"
"Dunno."
it's just boxing.

We signed a petition; worth it
stop women wearing skirts into the ring
Her footwork, flow, strength, ability, power,
speed, attitude her aura
inspiring…

something more powerful and exciting
flowing through the air.
immersed in a witnessing
a new turn for women's Olympic boxing

Boom! She wins her fight
optimistic energy flowing from her
spreading to each of us,
women, we stand united in this moment.

I feel something light inside me
and think to myself, "I could do that!"

Research in boxing has commonly found that it can enable a radical reinvention of the self (Gammel 2012; Wacquant 1995; Owton 2015). A phenomenologically-inspired approach to boxing via poetry seems well aligned given the focus on lived experience and the attempt to 'bring the body back in' (Allen-Collinson 2009a, p. 279). In this way, poetry can be employed in an attempt to capture the feelings, the sensuousness of fleshy experience and understand the person's *existential* grasp of the world (Leder 2001; Merleau-Ponty 1962; Owton 2015).

One could also employ poetry as data by utilising personal poetry written in the past. Furman (2004) reflected on poems he had written about his father's diagnosis of lung cancer. These were written a decade before and were employed in order to explore his reactions at various points in time. He seemed to address his sense of fragmentation in his life by writing poetry as a way to restore a better sense of order and balance. I worked similarly via writing about the loss of my own father (Owton 2012). In this sense, poetry can also be understood as a form of therapy which the Chap. 6 explores.

References

Allen-Collinson, J. (2009). Sporting embodiment sports studies and the (continuous) promise of phenomenology. *Qualitative Research in Sport and Exercise, 1*(3), 239–279.

Allen-Collinson, J., & Hockey, J. (2001). Runners' tales: Autoethnography, injury and narrative. *Auto/Biography, 9*(1&2), 95–106.

Bishop, E., & Willis, K. (2014). "Hope is that fiery feeling": Using poetry as data to explore the meanings of hope for young people. In *Forum qualitative Sozialforschung/Forum: Qualitative social research* (Vol. 15, No. 1). Available http://www.qualitative-research.net/index.php/fqs/article/view/2013/3631. Accessed 10 Apr 17.

Blinne, K. C. (2010). Writing my life: A narrative and poetic-based autoethnography. *Journal of Poetry Therapy, 23*(3), 183–190.

Drummond, D. K. (2017). The decision: A creative autoethnographic account with poetry. *Health Communication*, 1–3.

Eckersley, R., Cahill, H., Wierenga, A., & Wyn, J. (2007). *Generations in dialogue about the future: The hopes and fears of young Australians.* Canberra: Australia 21 Ltd. Melbourne: Australian Youth Research Centre.

Furman, R. (2004). Using poetry and narrative as qualitative data: Exploring a father's cancer through poetry. *Families, Systems, and Health, 22*(2), 162.

Furman, R. (2006). Autoethnographic poems and narrative reflections: A qualitative study on the death of a companion animal. *Journal of Family Social Work, 9*(4), 23–38.

Furman, R. (2007). Poetry and narrative as qualitative data: Explorations into existential theory. *Indo-Pacific Journal of Phenomenology, 7*(1), 1–9.

Gammel, I. (2012). Lacing up the gloves: Women, boxing and modernity. *Cultural and Social History, 9*(3),369–390.

Henderson, S. W. (2002). Medical student elegies: The poetics of caring. *Journal of Medical Humanities, 23*(2), 119–132.

King, T. (2003). *The truth about stories: A native narrative.* Toronto: House of Anansi.

Leder, D. (2001). Lived Body: A tale of two bodies: the Cartesian Corpse and the Lived Body. In D. Welton (Ed.). *Body and Flesh: A Philosophical Reader* (pp.117–129). Oxford: Blackwell.

Machado, S. (2016). Faggot speaks: A poetic inquiry into the experiences of antigay mistreatment and sexual prejudice. *Art/Research International: A Transdisciplinary Journal, 1*(1), 65–87.

Maurino, J. P. (2016). Transformations of the self: A narrative and poetic based autoethnography. *Journal of Poetry Therapy, 29*(4), 207–221.

Merleau-Ponty, M. (1962). *Phenomenology of perception.* London: Routledge.

Ngunjiri, F. W., Hernandez, K. A. C., & Chang, H. (2010). Living autoethnography: Connecting life and research. *Journal of Research Practice, 6*(1), 1.

Owton, H. (2012). Streams of bereavement. *Qualitative Inquiry, 20,* 1–4.

Owton, H. (2015) 'Reinventing the body-self: Intense, gendered and heightened sensorial experiences of women's boxing embodiment', in A. Channon, and C. Matthews (Eds.). *Global Perspectives on women in combatsport: Women Warriors around the world* (pp. 221–236). Basingstoke: Palgrave Macmillan. IBSN 978-1-137-43935-2

Owton, H. (2016). *A qualitative case study of sexual abuse in sport* (p. 109). Basingstoke: Palgrave Publishers. IBSN: 978-3319467955.

Owton, H., & Allen-Collinson, J. (2017). Athlete domestic violence: Contaminating acts and the violation of self-boundaries. In A. Milner & J. H. Braddock II (Eds.), *Women in sports: Breaking barriers, facing obstacles.* IBSN: 1-4408-5124-7.

Owton, H., & Sparkes, A. (2017). Sexual abuse and the grooming process in sport: Bella's story. *Sport, Education and Society.* Available http://www.tandfonline.com/doi/abs/10.1080/13573322.2015.1063484.

Piirto, J. (2002). The question of quality and qualifications: Writing inferior poems as qualitative research. *International Journal of Qualitative Studies in Education, 15*(4), 431–445.

Prendergast, M. (2009). Introduction: The phenomena of poetry in research: "Poem is what?" Poetic inquiry in qualitative social science research. In

M. Prendergast, C. Leggo and P. Sameshima (Eds.). *Poetic Inquiry: Vibrant voices in the social sciences* (pp. 13–29). Rotterdam: Sense Publishers

Shapiro, J. (2004). Can poetry be data? Potential relationships between poetry and research. *Families, Systems, and Health, 22*(2), 171–177.

Shapiro, J., & Stein, H. (2005). Poetic license: Writing poetry as a way for medical students to examine their professional relational systems. *Families, Systems, & Health, 23*(3), 278.

Wacquant, L. J. (1995). Pugs at work: Bodily capital and bodily labour among professional boxers. *Body & society, 1*(1), 65–93.

CHAPTER 4

Turning Data into Poetry

Abstract This chapter focuses on turning data into poetry which is commonly referred to as participant-voiced poems. Whilst there are many examples of 'completed' poems in Poetic Inquiry, there is less about the *process* of crafting a poem from interview data. In this section, examples will be used to show how to turn data (e.g. interviews) into poetry and offer clusters of poems focusing on various topics and themes throughout. Also, I include an example of a multi-voiced poem to show the different forms Poetic Inquiry can take.

Keywords Poetic analysis · Poetic clusters · Asthma · Pain · Chronic illness

Poetic Analysis Procedure

Leavy (2015) suggests that given the limited amount of words in poetry language should be '*razor sharp*'. In order to construct a poem, however, one needs to know what a poem is. The English word 'Poem' comes from the Greek noun *poiēma* meaning 'workmanship'. According to the Collins English Dictionary (2014), a poem is defined as:

> A composition in verse, usually characterised by concentrated and heightened language in which words are chosen for their sound and suggestive

H. Owton, *Doing Poetic Inquiry*, Palgrave Studies in Creativity and Culture, DOI 10.1007/978-3-319-64577-3_4

> power as well as for their sense, and using such techniques as metre, rhyme, and alliteration.

The definition includes prose poems as 'a literary composition that is not verse but exhibits the intensity of imagination and language common to it' and poetry as anything resembling a poem in beauty, effect, which is a rhythmically written expression of emotion or ideas in an arrangement of words/verse. Poetry is quite emotionally charged and intense which makes rhythm significant in poetry (Roberts 1995). What differentiates poetry from prose, however, are the various techniques, rhythm, rhyme, metaphor, imagery and repetition. The danger in writing poems using strict patterns of rhyme and meter, however, is that a poet-researcher might 'force' words into lines for the sake of such rules and might end up changing the *meanings* of the participant's narratives. Poetic Inquiry merges some of the rules of traditional poetry and the craft of writing with the beliefs of qualitative research (Leavy 2015). When I write participant-voiced poems ('Vox Participare') (Prendergast 2009), I work to extend or accentuate the *meaning* and the *concept* of the poem, as opposed to prioritising sound, rhyme and rhythm, particularly given the emphasis on the participants and their use of diction in the poem. Galvin and Todres (2009, p. 309) point out

> The re-presentation has to be able to connect to people in a heartfelt way and be complex enough to awaken not just a logical understanding, but also the sense of it as it lives. When it is living in this way, it is in excess for the words, and more than words can say.

In my research, I choose poetry to retell some people's stories, particularly because poetry allows the heart to lead the mind rather than the reverse and is aimed at authentically 'showing' the bond between us (Butler-Kisber and Stewart 2009; Pelias 2004). Turning data into poetry is where the words from the interview transcription are used to form the poem. Similarly to others (e.g. Richardson 2000; Douglas 2004), I adhere to the ethics of imposing rules on myself when constructing the poems. When I first started Poetic Inquiry, there was not a 'how to' guide for researchers to follow. Much Poetic Inquiry offered examples of completed poems as opposed to the *process* and seems to assume an attitude of intuition which appears necessary for many different types of qualitative research. Whilst (self) awareness is an important aspect for qualitative researchers, many novice researchers struggle to identify feelings about their research and scramble through the dark in an effort to grapple with these feelings once they are uncovered (Collins and Cooper 2014). Given the limited support offered to graduate students about the research process, like others (e.g. Leavy 2015), I offer a more substantial breakdown of the *process,* and I add to this literature by offering additional examples of participant-voiced poems.

The procedure of Poetic Inquiry involves reading and re-reading the transcripts over and over to gain a familiarity with the data. This is similar to coding and searching the transcript for themes. The poems can emerge from the transcript in ways that capture the '*whats*', '*whys*' and/or the '*hows*' of experience. Poindexter (2002) described her search for poetic representation by looking for unambiguous phrases, strong statements, eloquent expressions and wording that appealed to her. Likewise, I use the transcript to search for sections in the narrative that I feel strongly captures the feelings and emotions of the person I interview. I acknowledge that the poems are crafted by me where I make interpretations and decide how the poem will be constructed, choosing which words and how it takes shape. I may weigh up changing the order of someone's words so that it may rhyme *if* the opportunity is there, as long as this does not change or 'distort' the meaning of their experience.

I draw from an example of research I conducted with sportspeople with asthma exploring the embodied experiences of breathing. Here is an example of how I might craft someone's interview data into a poetic text:

J: *if I'm getting stressed* and *I'm rushing around*, then I, *I do start coughing*, and *just every now and again*, they get *really* it, it takes over, *my husband will say, look just sit down and just you know, let it happen* and it *becomes a sort of coughing fit.* Not so often recently, but it has sometimes got uncomfortable and quite bad.

H: Hmmm, yeah and your husband, he sounds like he looks after you then?

J: Well, he, yes he does. He knows, he knows me well and my, my family too, if I start coughing, they'll say, *Mum just go and sit down,* just, just don't try and to, that's what they say, *stop talking mum, just don't talk* [laughing]. And, and just *relax* and I think it is, it's probably *training to relax the throat muscles* and just, not, not keep, *I try to keep going and you have to just stop and let it, let it sort of die itself out.*

This part of the conversation was then crafted into the following verse in one of her poems:

If I'm rushing around, getting stressed,
I start coughing; just every now and again,
My husband will say, *"Look just sit down, let it happen!"*
Becoming a sort of coughing fit,
"Mum just go and sit down,
stop talking, just don't talk Mum!"
Relax; training to relax the throat muscles,
I try to keep going; you have to just stop and let it,
let it sort of die itself out…

Through this crafting into poetry, one may also notice the significant reduction in words whilst also maintaining the meaning. As Mallarme (1896, online, 30 March 2012) says, 'it is the job of poetry to clean up our word-clogged reality by creating silences around things'. Given the obsession with language that often accompanies qualitative researchers, the reduction of word content appears to be quite a vantage point. In addition, at times, the size of the font and placing of sentences can be adapted to visually enhance the meaning of the written text although some argue that this can be slightly off-putting. It is important to remember that too much interference with a poem could prove pointless. As Wilde (1972, p. 72) states, 'I was working on the proof of one of my poems all the morning, and took out a comma. In the afternoon I put it back again'.

What I show next is clusters of *Asthma*; *Chronic Illnesses; Injured male athletes.*

Cluster of Asthma Poems

Gunge

Awful gunge…
I feel like I want to put something down my throat,
Draw it all of it out.
Gunge, the worst thing
This coughing,
Sometimes I wake up
it's in my throat,
it wakes you up…

it's not so much the coughing,
it's the stuff that's there...
To be honest, I've never really known a great deal about it,
The gunge, that collects....
People far worse with asthma than *me,*
I'm an old person, something that comes with age,
I've never had it.
I never had it before.
I don't know that it was diagnosed at the time,
it must have been then
I can remember having this *gunge* in my throat.

That's the only reason for it, really.

I'll settle for that

you can get quite concerned really,
you mustn't get worried
you have to keep calm
you mustn't get all uptight over it

sometimes it's quite worrying
can't get your breath sometimes
it's not really very terrible really.
it's better than some things

I could never live without it.
I thought well I've settle for that.
If I've gotta have something,
I'll settle for that.

Takes a while

step out from a really warm room, fire on
step out into winter conditions,
takes your breath away,
It's like that all the time.

Sport; battling, constantly aware
the way you're breathing
the air
your mouth and nose covered

cling film, carrier bag,
a few tiny pin pricks in it
let the air in.
It's like that. Takes a while.

the air's there, can get it in,
getting it out takes so long
gasping
get the air back in

breathing out against something that's on your face
a few holes,
takes a while, takes a while,
stop; level out again, takes a while.

My daughters

Run, cough, cough - sick
I hear coughing in their bed
cough, cough, cough, barf

my shit genetics passing on
mucking about, coughing, coughing
they're young

Night-time; lying down, cough, cough, cough
lots of coughing, coughing until she's sick
not good, seeing her being sick

don't like that

I'd sooner they didn't have asthma,
bit beastly,
a tight life

monitor; see how it goes.

Coughing; blue inhaler
we do that.
they're cool

pretty tough; a puff of an inhaler
before they could do anything,
kids; play happens at any moment

my asthma, *thinking* more about asthma
because of them.

I don't remember it

I don't know what happens.
I can't tell you.

through thin straws, breathing
clothes peg on your nose,
go running with that

I don't remember

I can't tell you what happens
when I have an asthma attack
I just don't know at all.

I couldn't tell you sorry

difficult to breathe out
You get the air in,
you can't get it out

I don't know

difficult to breathe in
lungs; carbon dioxide
you can't get it out

It's like that

feeling out of breath
I remember feeling really tight
I remember trying to pull my shirt from my neck
going outside

next thing; back in an ambulance
transferred

I get *told* all of this
I remember I've been told it,
well I don't remember it,

I remember what they tell me.

Part of me

Unusual to have brittle asthma,
A label used; getting sympathy,
Some people I find annoying,
"I've got brittle asthma"
Well, no you don't; you're on 1 tablet and 1 inhaler,
You don't know what you're on about,
You really *don't* have brittle asthma.

Part of life; doesn't define me,
Part of me is quite proud to have asthma,
Met loads of people; asthma ambassador.
Bonuses; definitely don't outweigh the negatives,
I don't know what life is without it so it's actually
part of me, it always has been, always will be.
Gotta live, make the *most* of your situation,
No point wallowing, wasting your life away, feeling sorry.
I'm not disabled,
I can do anything you do, I just have to do it a different way,
I'm not disabled.
I want to do what I'm not allowed to do; what I'm not advised to do,
Like rebelling; don't want to admit that you're as ill as you actually are,
I don't smoke a lot; just through drunkenness,
Not often; not a huge amount; it's enough I guess.
Not proud of it, something that happens, I guess.

In and out of hospital

Diagnosed at 3; youngest age you can be,
Inhaler; like a spaceship. Not traumatic,
Expected I would have it.
I've been in control of it; myself, I manage it.
At school; really *unusual* to have asthma.

Couldn't count the number of admissions in and out of hospital,
Took me a while to realise; my limits knowing, get back in control,
Doctor's warning; next asthma attack will kill me,
Taking stock; now behaving,
Now I know… learning,

I just do what I feel able to be doing,
I won't do it to the point; when you've finished playing,
"Oh my goodness, I'm gonna die."
I don't do it to that level; behaving,
Leaving Uni; long distance learning,
Just have to be careful about planning things.

Weather; preparedness.
Can't be spontaneous; just the little things,
Inhalers; swallowing 10 tablets; nebulisers, takes 20 min,
I don't like it.
I worry about what it will do to my system,

What would I prefer?
Taking all that and being able to breathe?
Or not taking it and not being able to breathe?
Used to it now,
Not a big thing.

The poems show various themes about asthma, identity, embodiment and disruption that are not always readily available or easily conveyed in more traditional methods. Asthma is about breathing (or struggling with it) but breathing is primarily an unconscious function and we will inhale approximately twelve to fourteen times per minute without even *thinking* about it (Marieb and Hoehn, 2007). Breathing is fundamental in all walks of life and to control one's breathing when engaged in sport becomes even more important (Marieb and Hoehn 2007).

It seems that as long as participants are able to breathe freely and easily, the body disappears from their conscious awareness. As Leder (1990) explains, to disappear in this sense is simply not to appear. Breathing is usually automatic and a taken-for-granted action and when the body breathes freely and lets the flow of air into and out of the lungs, the body poses no problem or threat. The breathing body is temporarily absent of asthma and hence of disease (disease—in Leder's terms 1990), and so there is no discomfort or physiological disruption; their body self represents a state of health. For these participants, the body is never a simple presence, like asthma is never a simple presence, but that which is away from itself, a being of difference and absence (Leder 1990).

Coughing, wheezing or gunge seem to give way to this dys-appearance (Leder 1990). Noises and symptoms associated with asthma disrupt the flow of breathing, which has an impact on participants' sport and their life. This also might interfere with and threaten their identity as an athlete and specifically their self-perception as a 'fit' athlete. Asthmatic bodies are no longer alien-as-forgotten, but as contingent and threatening bodies (Leder 1990) and remembered and reminded through asthmatic bodily experiences. The poems are participants' words and convey images, emotion and disruption in relation to bodily experiences of asthma and sport; indeed showing that the body is central to understanding (Allen-Collinson and Owton 2014, 2015).

Unexpected and Unanticipated Turns

Different things can arise in conversation and through reflective interviewing participants can make links between various events in their lives. One of the joys of qualitative research is the unexpected and unanticipated turns that research can take when you travel alongside your participants. Poetry allows for these complexities to sit with each other. The following poem emerged out of research with sportspeople with asthma. My participant was reflecting on why and when asthma emerged in her life. This took her back to some deeper issues which she reflected on in the interview. When I was doing my PhD, I had not expected this sort of thing to arise but was prepared for it. In her history, she divulged a history of suffering domestic abuse as well. Here, the poem 'I still Struggle' shows how she had bulimia and still struggles to work through it.

I still struggle

problems with breathing
Hay fever; bad bulimia too,

I maintained weight,
Being sick, not eating; faddy things.

Ridiculous weights, too skinny,
didn't help

3 years, I've not had bulimia,
touch wood,

a little bit after baby was born,
longer actually.... it is longer.

I got a bit of you know baby weight,
I do still struggle; joined a proper club,

getting into a bit of a state about it,
'Okay it's 5 o'clock, it's food time, what am I going to eat?'

obsessed about what I eat,
Since joining slimming world,

a state about things,
may sound *'ahhh, I'm obsessive about sins'*
it isn't.

I eat more,
I eat loads

healthy things,
actually lose weight still

I'm in a different mindset now,
I am happy

slim gorgeous girls
They've all some kind of eating disorders

They're talking to me about it,
I'm thinking...

'I'm not the best person to talk about this'

Fighting Pain

These poems take a more narrative style. Sometimes, as opposed to a theme, you might want to capture a story. The following poem was crafted from research with sportspeople with asthma and whilst asthma features in it, he talks about how sport pushed him to carry on after he was in a car crash that hit him out of nowhere. I wanted to maintain and capture the intensity of his fight with pain which is why this poem is longer.

I'm going to beat it

After neck operation,
The Great North Run,
Body harness, neck brace on,
Quarter of a pint of morphine; pumped full of medication,
Pockets full of gel with coated ginger,
Frenzied determination.

Good decision?
No, medically,
Mentally – definitely,
To impress Mummy and Daddy,
To *achieve*, *to feel* better,
the *purpose* drags me on.

Now, fascinated,
Asthma; how much it has sportingly affected,
Could I run without getting out of breath?
I don't know; it's been a while,
It sets off my head,
Big distractions needing; pain overcoming,
Always a challenge to be having.

I intend to run a marathon,
Only for a reason,
I will *try* a triathlon,
And am going to walk across the Pyrenees,
One side to the other,
Who knows…
                    the effect on neck pain and asthma.
Guess I'll find out doing,
Stop me? Nothing!
Bit slower; lying,
First one across the Pyrenees crawling.

Against doctor's wishing,
Loving a bit of competing,
With everything,
Not meant to be doing,
With asthma; not breathing,
Neck's spasming; Pain it is making,
"Well don't DO anything"
So I nearly punched him!

Competitive spirit,
Gets me through it,
I have to *beat* it,
I could just lie down; give into it,
Be a bum. No. I'm going to beat it,
For *me;* I want to be better than this,

Somehow…

Even if I have to cut me own neck off…

Next operation
Solve me
or
kill me
Who knows?

But now
talking about this
is making me sad.

Clusters of Chronic Illness

During my asthma research, many other chronic illnesses arose in discussions. The following clusters are of participants' narratives of rare conditions and experiences in and around various chronic illnesses (e.g. unknown illnesses, *Ménière's,* and stroke).

Granny's Memoirs II
I thought I was going to die

Bells ringing, people looking,
Awful feeling; I didn't know what was happening,

Bit confusing; students kept saying,
"*It, it's alright, don't worry, don't worry*"
Wanting me to stay in; I wouldn't.

Grandpa never rang
He might have shown *some* interest!
I was a bit cross; put out,
I can remember so well.

Picking him up at the station,
"*I'm going into hospital on Saturday*"
That shook him I can tell you!
Hospital; took me up on the Saturday,
I reckon I was a guinea pig actually.

I quite, quite, *quite* thought I was going to die,
I thought I was getting ready to die,
It didn't worry me you see; funny,
Capable of looking after themselves, family.

I was gonna live - quite happy,
Thought I was going to die, honestly,
I was going to die,
I didn't get into tears about it,
I suppose it's all part of the illness really.

Piggy eyed, feet like balloons, all blown up,
Horrible; a haemorrhage
Fell asleep everywhere,
I couldn't keep awake.

Guy's; wheeled in
Outpatient for a year,
Photographed for the Lancet; my hands, my feet, everything,
Never actually saw them,
I wasn't a doctor really was I?

They didn't want me to come out,
Myself; Discharged,
Holiday, on the train,
Most nightmareish thing I've ever done.

Shut away in a hospital,
Another world,
All of a sudden,
In all this traffic; dreadful,
I was horrified.

Year later…
Guy's rang; Very interested
invited as a patient privately,
Students to see the results of all that they'd done on me,

I reckon that I was a guinea pig in those days.

I did, I did do it actually,
I didn't mind a bit; they thanked me,
I did help somebody, someone on the way,
'*I helped somebody as I walked along the road*' as they say

A long job; worth it,
Nothing was horrible really,
Happy to be alive really,
50, 60 years ago wouldn't happen today,
Much more advanced.

Very disturbed for a long time,
I've been on that medication ever since,
"*Never to go without it*"
I don't.

I can almost rattle with pills,
I don't care. I'm here.
"*It's no fun is it getting old*" People say,
"*Well I'm still going, I'm glad I'm here,*
I've got 7 grandchildren, 9 great grandchildren,
I love it" I say.

It came on the Friday morning

It came on the Friday morning,
Out of bed, downstairs,
Breakfast, all normal,

Went to the toilet, upstairs,
Went to get off the toilet,
My right leg wouldn't work anymore,
Grabbed the side of the bath, I did,
Had a few dead legs before,
Didn't really think about it.

Into my shower; I couldn't stand,
I *YELLED*,
My wife came up, gave me a hand,
Got me out, *"What's the matter?"*
"Well my legs have just collapsed"
Got washed, dressed, sat in the front room, rang the doctor,
Wasn't *my* doctor; a different doctor,
"You *sound* alright"
"I feel alright"
I said,
"Feels like someone's *kicked* me in the leg"
Two alternatives: *Ambulance; straight to hospital,*
If you feel up to it come in and see me this afternoon,
That's what I did.

I said to my wife, *"I'd like a cup of coffee"*
She made a cup of coffee,
"What are you doing?" She said to me,
"Toilet" I want to go,
"You couldn't walk a minute ago"
I drove *myself* to see the doctor; examined me,
"Nothing wrong; you *may* have had a TIA",
Like a warning,
gave me some aspirin,
sent me on my way.

Tesco; driving, did all the shopping,
Came home, did some cooking,
I always cook a meal on a Friday night,
Went to bed,
That was it.

Woke up Saturday,
Leg wouldn't work *again*,
"It'll be alright by lunchtime won't it?"

It wasn't.

Sunday, I went to get out of bed,
I collapsed, only half collapsed really,
The legs wouldn't support me,
My wife got me to hospital,
Transferred me Monday,
Physiotherapist came to see me

Two hours, moving my muscles,
Moved to the stroke ward Tuesday,
They gave me a frame to walk around, up and down,
Wanted a program from the physiotherapist,
I've been *active* all my life! Always exercising,
I *showed* her what I was doing,
Went *BERSERK* didn't she,
"It's better to do something correctly 10 times than 100 times wrongly"
Gave me a stick Wednesday; home on Friday,
Stick in the corner; haven't used it since,
Dependence.

I'm going to do something physical,
Get out some aggression; not hitting people,
Stroke group, 3 years now,
I love it; excellent, very, very good progression.

I can't play squash, I can't go skiing,
If you look at somebody else of 72,
You don't expect to be playing competitive squash do you?
That's the way I look at it
Driving, go abroad, do lots of walking,
Just getting physical, exercise helps with things.

No, I don't really listen to my body now; never listened before either,
I'm in control; mind over matter,
My problem; I push myself higher
than I should,

I'm now getting older,
Muscles not as strong now as they were,
I've now got a heart monitor,
Set it to a level; with a beeper,

I push myself; I know I do it,
I always have done,
There's no reason for it,
but there we are,
No good worrying about things is it?

Dizzy

First happened, 2 or 3 years ago,
Time to time; dizzy,
uncomfortable and dizzy,
Inside I felt very uncomfortable; sick,
In the kitchen I sat, feeling very unwell,
Bed; I got undressed
I needed help.

I wanted my son.

Downstairs, my phone,
That was difficult,
In the downstairs loo; sick,
I felt awful, frightened,
I very, very, rarely vomit
I should have phoned for medical help,
I wasn't thinking straight…

I phoned my son.

He arrived; he took charge,
Immensely relieved,
Paramedic arrived; he didn't talk to me,
I could hear everything,
I remember him saying,
"Caw, look at those eyes, they're all over the place."
In the downstairs loo; sick again

Very vivid memories; Traumatic
Stands out for me,
Wonderful and capable help my son gave me,
The Menniers
never been as bad

I haven't vomited again; sometimes felt sick with it,
often dizzy.

Medication; I take daily
Nuisance; not as traumatic as that first big one,
In between bouts, I get on with my life, cycle and walk
I make sure I have medication with me just in case.
it really doesn't interfere with normal daily life
going to the gym 3 times a week,
cycling into town to shop,
walking the 2 collies

I am fit and healthy

Cultural understandings of chronic illnesses have been neglected in much research, particularly in sporting subcultures (Owton 2013). People may deal with their symptoms in ways that reflect cultural attitudes embedded in sport (Owton 2013). For example, sportspeople may ignore, diminish, minimise or hide symptoms; therefore a focus on analysing why they adopt such perspectives may assist in understanding people's sporting engagement and experiences of chronic illness. Some participants seem to want to avoid feeling like a burden and therefore take personal responsibility for their illnesses by trying to minimise the disruption to other people's lives; further highlighting another relational element of illness experiences. These poems highlight these aspects, embracing the silences and the gaps which allow for interpretive understandings.

Cluster of Injured Males

The following cluster of poems emerged from the research I conducted with injured males. Semi-structured interviews (30–40 mins) were conducted and tape-recorded with three male athletes who had experienced sporting injuries and surgery as a result of these injuries. The semi-structured nature also allowed the respondents the opportunity to develop ideas that were important to them. Whilst much research has been conducted with men, sport, masculinity and injury, there seems to be little poetry on the topic. Here, I include a poem transcribed from Tim's interview data 'Learning to walk again' and a poem transcribed from Mike's interview data 'Confessions of an addict' to capture men's experiences of injury and sport.

Learning to walk again (Tim)

In the army; from a broken home actually,
At 16, basketball; my reason to be,
England under 21 squad,
Fantastic. I really enjoyed it,
260 medals; basketball was *everything* for me,
That's all I did; basketball was my life,
My wife; her support made it a lot easier, psychologically.

Post player; get bumped a lot,
Bone cut off my hip,
Blink of back pain terrific!
Bone growth on my spine,
Pressing down on my sciatic nerve,
Wonderful medical treatment in army,
Harley street specialist flew out to Germany.

Operation; very, very well,
Comeback; horrific,
Wheelchair; walking again learning,
Absolutely horrendous; scar tissue, pain shooting,
Stand up; absolutely excruciating.
A very long
gradual process.

A very hard process
a year,
a whole year.

I used to get down a bit,
No light at the end of the tunnel,
A lot of encouragement from family and physio,
"You can do this, come on, think about what you went through,
how hard you used to play, you can do it"
All wanted to see me comeback; comrades, my friends,
All that encouragement fantastic.

Army wants you fit,
Comeback quick.
Basketball's always been my reason to be,

"Do I really want to become just an armchair sportsman
sit around, watch TV, or do I want to get back to this"
In the back of my mind; kept me going,

Eventually; full fitness,
Couldn't *wait*; immediately back playing,
Lower level; more teams, more playing,
4 more years playing...

The truth - I overdid it.

Physio, "*This is the time to stop.*"
Pain; muscular damage, scar tissue,
Like all sportsmen; playing was more important to me,
Lived with that.
Eventually, too much to bear,
'If you keep playing, you're going to end up seriously injured in a wheel-chair'

It's time to stop.

Absolutely devastating,
Basketball's my life,
Coaching - no buzz
Now, a referee,
Refereed on television,
Different kind of satisfaction,
Replaced the buzz, I really, really enjoy it.

Still miss playing,
It's not worth the risk.
I still pass the under 30's fitness test at 54,
It's given me a reason to keep going.

Passing on; I'm always saying,
"If you've got an injury, treat it right, STOP playing"
One referee friend; an ankle injury,
He's comeback; after every time he plays,
Swells up doesn't it,
'You've got to take a month out and rest it'
Best lesson I've learned,
As much as you love what you do,

Let the injury heal properly,
Playing through the injury; worse you'll make it,
You'll end up losing the thing you love the most,
Big lesson that I learned out of it.

Confessions of an addict (Mike)

Always been into sports,
Basketball; National league team.

I snapped my ACL,
My left knee, it really hurt
Put me out for a couple of years,
Never been quite the same since.

Hospital,
"It's a sprain, give it a couple of weeks rest"
Gave it a couple of weeks rest,
Kept on resting it, going back.
It really hurt.

Knee brace *"I'll just play with this knee brace on"*
It just hurt.

A year later,
"Oh you've snapped your anterior crucial ligament"
It was painful when I was playing,
"Oh well it's only a sprain" I was thinking,
You just sort of play through it don't you.

Took them another year; operation.
2 years wasted
Massive scar on my knee,
6 inches long,
Now – all keyhole surgery.

Physio twice a week,
"You won't be able to play for 9 months"
Played 8 weeks after the operation,
bit silly - it was important

That was painful,
It hurt,
We won,
That's all that's important.

Too old now, I should be stopping,
Ignore it when you're playing,
Afterwards, "*Ahhhh have to stop playing!*"
I just ice it.

I shouldn't be playing,
No point in resting,
Better; the more you keep it moving.

"*You'll stop playing after this won't you*" family worry,
I won't,
fat lumps sat on the sofa,
I don't wanna do that.

I dunno what I'd do if I didn't do basketball,
I've been paying for so long,
37. A long time; part of your life,
The whole team thing

If I walked away from it altogether,
It would be like someone dying.

Participants described a long-life history attachment to their sport in that they had 'always been into sports' (Mike). Sport was where they experienced enjoyment and fun with friends, which supplemented their social life. The enjoyment was enhanced by feelings of competency and the investment of hard work, which satisfied their sense of achievement. Therefore, sport appeared to be a significant part of their lives that was strongly related to their sense of identity. Tim describes how 'basketball sort of became my reason to be', however, all the participants had been forced or were in the process of facing the prospect of withdrawing from their sports due to their injuries. Their active sporting self was situated in the past, and they appeared to be in the process of reordering their identities following their injuries. Mike stated how since the injury he has, 'never been quite the same since' but the thought of walking away from his sport altogether 'would be like someone dying'.

In desperate attempts to cling on to their sporting selfs, participants played regardless of their injury and against medical advice. For example, Mike described a situation where he played very soon after his operation after being told not to play for 9 months, 'I actually played 8 weeks after the operation [laughs]. Which was a bit silly. But it was important'. In the poem, playing sport and winning were more important than his physical well-being. It appeared that he was willing to accept the consequences of playing injured. This also demonstrated how playing sport was extremely important to his sense of being. Participants expressed a fear of becoming physically inactive. Mike had a fear of turning 'into fat lumps sat on the sofa'. This sense of denial demonstrated the difficulty these men had in accepting their injuries and the possibility of never being able to play sport again. As a result, the injury appeared to threaten the attachment to their identities as physically able bodied males. Instead, these men felt the need to state and demonstrate comebacks to sport, quickly and without complaint (Tim).

Often, men who are brought up in an environment emphasising masculine ideals through previous sporting experiences appear to be more resilient to pain due to a more natural 'mentally tough' attitude. This masculinising experience seems to encourage a 'win-at-all costs' mentality. This can be detrimental to further damage, given that Mike believed that further damage to his newly operated on the knee was worth risking due to the importance he placed on winning. The Pain was endured and readily accepted as a result of actually participating in sport. The main messages that the poems seem to portray are the importance of self-care and looking after our bodies when injured.

Multi-voice Poetry

As Poetic Inquiry gains credence, researchers are starting to experiment more with different types of Poetic Inquiry. Leavy (2009, 2010) refers to tri-voiced poems as a way to combine original data, existing literature and autoethnographic researcher observations. When combining more voices, we can term these as 'multi-voiced'. Multi-voice poetry is a poem involving more than one voice and seems to have some similarities with ethnodrama which has been described as 'dramatizing the data' (Saldaña 2005, p. 2). An ethnodrama is known as the performance 'text' and then it shifts to ethnotheatre when it is performed. The following poem is an example of a multi-voiced poem from the research I conducted with sportspeople with asthma. This poem is an attempt to capture the combined multifaceted essences of medicalised experiences of asthma from 11 different voices.

Doctors

[Voice 1]
I went to the doctor,
he tested me,
he said to me,
you have a chest etcetera,
Basically came to the conclusion,
I had asthma,
I had to take an inhaler,
2 puffs in the morning,
2 puffs in the evening.
Chest infections,
Back to the doctor's,
Get it cleared,
Generally speaking,
It has no effect at all,
i.e. it's under control isn't it.

[Voice 2]
I get wheezy for several days a week,
for several consecutive weeks,
what I did do previously
highly un-recommended by the GPs,
I'd just increase my own dose
if that didn't work then I'd go and see them
I've been able to manage it quite well
I have always been keen to want to,
once it is stable and managed to try and reduce the dose of whatever
I'm on as much as possible.
They recommend that you *don't* self medicate
might be to, to protect people from taking too much
I'm quite aware of the maximum prescribed effective dose
If you take more it's not gonna help you anymore

[Voice 3]
Doctor's didn't take me seriously,
Now, they agree I have asthma,

Asthma clinic, the sister nurse,
"*How are you?*" she said,
"*Fine*" I said,
"*Accept from this gunge I get in my throat*"
"*oh I think we can do something about that now*" she said,
She gets the book out,
it's the nurse, not the doctor,
She gets the book out, looks up this name,
'*I must go, clear it with the doctor's first*
as to whether it's okay for you to take it' She said,
She was gone for a long time,
I thought she'd got lost!
she came back, "*It was okay*" she said,
So she gave me the tablets.

[Voice 4]
I spent 3 months going back to the nurse,
having to sleep upright…
every night,
as soon as I lay down
I just coughed and coughed and coughed…
after 3 months of going to see the nurse,
she finally then said, '*I think you should now see the doctor*'
by that time of course I needed antibiotics,
I was not very happy about that,
3 months I was like that.
I went on holiday,
just couldn't sleep,
as soon as I lay down,
I just coughed and coughed and coughed…
I take my inhalers now,
I don't wanna get like that again.

[Voice 5]
After my 2nd pregnancy
During pregnancy actually,
7 years now,
I developed really bad hay fever,
Hay fever caused me to have really bad pains in my chest,
I got really wheezy,
Very difficult to breathe,
I went to the doctor's about it,

Prescribed me with these 2 inhalers,
I don't know the difference between the 2 inhalers,
I know I have to take a puff of both of them for some reason,
I don't know why.
Hay fever was brought on…
by pregnancy, I presume,
I'm not 100% sure about that,
Doctor just said that strange things happened when you're pregnant.

[Voice 6]
I was told when I was young that you grow out of asthma,
it doesn't seem to be the case with me,
I seem to be growing right into it
blooming into this stage.

[Voice 7]
They said to me, '*oh it's alright, you can manage it*'
I didn't know what I was in for really,
They said, '*oh how old are you, hmmm nearly 14,*
you might grow out of it. It happens in 7's'
So I was like,
'*oh okay, right, didn't work this time, when am I 21?*
Okaaaay, mark that down on the calendar…
People tend to grow out of it in multiples of 7 years,
I didn't.
Yeah lots of little harsh hopes that it might go away
it didn't.
I suppose I didn't really think it would make any difference,
I wasn't really aware that it would make any difference,
I didn't know what would happen,
Asthma's an annoyance.

[Voice 8]
Brittle asthma; late onset,
Looked at sadly; doctors telling people,
"Well you haven't had it before and now you have"
Slightly *unusual* asthma; aspirin intolerable.
Doctor suggesting alternatives; experimentation,
I rarely say I may have asthma,
Not really noticeable any longer,
GP was a naughty experimenter!
Rather than sticking to the books ever.

[Voice 9]
In and out of hospital; another asthma attack,
Transferred; 2 paramedics, a doctor, intensive care nurse, intensive care doctor,
We all got to the ward, "*She's not very well, look at everyone she's got with her*",
Everyone there waiting,
Hands on his hips, "*What have you done now?*" joking,
I know I'm special; I get to see the prof!

[Voice 10]
Advice? They didn't really.
They were just like, '*take it when you need it.*
Take it twice a day. Twice at night, twice in the morning'
That was it,
they didn't really,
they just said, '*Just take it when you need it*'
I think that sometimes, '*oh yeah you've got asthma*'
sometimes they might be in a rush to diagnose it
'*here's an inhaler, go away*'
That's sort of how I felt.
I went back to the nurse..,
Every couple of months,
I'd get my peak flow read
I had to keep a peak flow chart when it first started,
they didn't really do much,
They just sort of looked at it and that was it.
To be honest,
I don't really feel like I got any advice from the doctor's,
Apart from '*just take it*'.
when they did look at your peak flow reading in the doctor's office,
the stuff that he was saying to me; a waste of time,
obviously *they* knew what it meant,
I was only quite young at the time,
I was like, '*Well is someone gonna explain it to me?*'
I didn't really get an explanation,
yeah I just felt,
just sort of brushed off.

[Voice 11]
Struggling with all things I'm not meant to be doing,
One doctor said to me, '*well don't do anything*'

so… I nearly punched him,
with lack of understanding,
about the world's life, all the bear it is.
I said, *'well hand me the tablets, I'll die now then'*
well, he meant it!
He said *'Well just don't do anything'*.
Whereas other doctors I've seen,
they've been such like,
'well bloody do it… suffer the consequences'
Very different techniques,
Some just want to fill you with drugs,
others want to inject you with things,
some want you to have no medication; just think about it.

Doctors and medical professionals can learn a great deal from patients' perspectives. Since four B.C. personal narratives have helped inform medical practitioners, but appeared to become increasingly marginalised during the nineteenth and twentieth centuries. Seneca (C. 4 B.C.–A.D.65), Floyer (1968), Proust (1871–1922), Brookes (1994) and Jackson (2005) are amongst those who have provided biographical and personal accounts of asthma. One significant figure who does not seem to have gained much attention in relation to his asthma is Ché Guevara (1928–1967). He did not offer personal accounts of his asthma; however, research into his biography has revealed interesting elements (The Gale Group 2004). Autobiographies and life histories on chronic illness are slowly becoming more commonplace again (Ellis 1995) and describe the more subjective experiences, like these poems, which can be accompanied by complex ethical dynamics (Ellis 2007).

References

Allen-Collinson, J., & Owton, H. (2014). Take a deep breath: Asthma, sporting embodiment, the senses, and 'auditory work'. *International Review for the Sociology of Sport, 49*(5), 592–608.

Allen-Collinson, J., & Owton, H. (2015). Intense embodiment: Senses of heat in women's running and boxing. *Body and Society, 21*(2), 245–268.

Brookes, T. (1994). *Catching my breath.* New York: Times Books.

Butler-Kisber, L., & Stewart, M. (2009). The use of poetry clusters in poetic inquiry. In M. Prendergast, C. Leggo, & P. Sameshima (Eds.), *Poetic inquiry* (pp. 3–12). Boston: Sense Publishers.

Collins English Dictionary. (2014). *Complete and unabridged* (12th ed.). New York: Harper Collins.

Collins, C. S., & Cooper, J. E. (2014). Emotional intelligence and the qualitative researcher. *International Journal of Qualitative Methods, 13*(1), 88–103.

Douglas, K. (2004). My Dad. Leanne, A poetic representation. In *Motivation and persistence in women professional tournament golfers* (pp. 187–207). Unpublished Doctoral Dissertation, University of Bristol.

Ellis, C. (1995). *Final negotiations: A story of love, loss and chronic illness.* Philadelphia: Temple University Press.

Ellis, C. (2007). Telling secrets, revealing lives: Relational ethics in research with intimate others. *Qualitative Research, 13*(1), 3–29.

Floyer J. (1968). *A treatise of the asthma* (pp. 7–8). London: R Wilkin and W Innys.

Galvin, K., & Todres, L. (2009). *Poetic enquiry and phenomenological research: The practice of 'embodied interpretation'* (pp. 307–316). Boston: Sense Publishers.

Jackson, M. (2005). *Asthma: A biography*. Oxford: Oxford University Press.

Leavy, P. (2009). Fractured femininities/massacred masculinities: A poetic installation. *Qualitative Inquiry, 15*(9), 1439–1447.

Leavy, P. (2010). Poetic bodies: Female body image, sexual identity and arts-based research. *Learninglandscapes, 4*(1), 175–187.

Leavy, P. (2015). *Method meets art: Arts-based research practice.* New York: Guilford Publications.

Leder, D. (1990). *The absent body*. Chicago: University of Chicago Press.

Mallarme, S. (1896). Modernist poet Mallarme. [Online 3 March 2012]. Available: http://article.wn.com/view/2012/03/30/Modernist_poet_Mallarme_now_in_Hebrew/. Accessed 24 Sep 2012.

Marieb, E. N., & Hoehn, K. (2007). Human anatomy & physiology. Pearson Education.

Owton, H. (2013). Integrating multiple forms of representation: Fighting asthma. *Qualitative Inquiry, 19*, 601–604.

Pelias, R. (2004). *A methodology of the heart: Evoking academic and daily life.* Walnut Creek, CA: AltaMira Press.

Poindexter, C. (2002). Research as poetry: A couple experiences HIV. *Qualitative Inquiry, 8*, 707–714.

Prendergast, M., 2009. Introduction: The phenomena of poetry in research: "Poem is what?" Poetic Inquiry in qualitative social science research. *Poetic Inquiry: Vibrant voices in the social sciences* (pp. 13–29).

Richardson, L. (2000). Writing: A method of inquiry. In N. Denzin & Y. Lincoln (Eds.), *Handbook of qualitative research* (2nd ed., pp. 923–948). London: Sage.

Roberts, E. (1995). *Writing about literature* (8th ed.). Upper Saddle River, NJ: Prentice Hall.

Saldaña, J. (2005). *Ethnodrama: An anthology of reality theatre* (Vol. 5). Lanham, MD: Rowman Altamira.
The Gale Group. (2004). *Guevara, Ché (Ernesto): 1928–1967: Revolution leader.* Available: http://www.encyclopedia.com/people/history/cuban-history-biographies/che-guevara. Accessed 26 Apr 2017.
Wilde, O. (1972). *The Story of an unhappy friendship: With portraits and facsimile letters.* London: The Hermes Press.

CHAPTER 5

Poetry as Literature Review

Abstract This chapter outlines other forms of poetry, specifically, how to create poems conceptually. This can be a helpful reflective task for researchers, and examples show how poems can *show* a concept which can be difficult to understand but if done well, a poem could help others to resonate with. Again, examples will be included from author's own work to show how to do this. For example, the imposter syndrome, experienced by many in academia, can be transformed into a poem which helps others to resonate with, and I break this down in order to show how this might enhance self-understanding.

Keywords Literature review · Poet-researchers · Academia

Sometimes, trying to understand a concept or reading through various research papers can feel overwhelming during a Ph.D.. During my Ph.D., I found the endless amount of reading engulfing at times.

Paper

Feeling deeply immersed in papers,
Seeing nothing past,
Continuously wading through piles; never tapers.
As I finish reading pieces float to the ground,

H. Owton, *Doing Poetic Inquiry*, Palgrave Studies in Creativity and Culture, DOI 10.1007/978-3-319-64577-3_5

Looking around my room; some are screwed up,
None make a sound.

Messy, unreadable; scribbled all over,
Easy to read; going with the flow, hence,
Some I read drunk; some I read sober,
Difficult, challenging; don't always make sense.

Some are typed; some pieces are written by hand,
Some are joined with other pieces,
Piles on piles; sinking in sand.

Sifting through a maze of phrases,
Metaphors, symbols, creating images,
Sublimating romantic, aggressive or nihilistic impulses,
In a dominating "disembodied" style of life,
Desire for decorporatising existence.

Too hot to handle; too cold to save,
Just break the silence from the body 'part',
Feeling the pen scribble over the page,
Physically out of control of the paper,
Exposing the inside of a poet's heart.

This leads me to discuss how poetry can help unravel concepts that might not be readily understood without writing creatively about it. Indeed, part of our jobs as academics is to make the complicated, simple and writing poetically about a concept could help you in the process of understanding complicated ideas or enhance understanding of yourself via a concept. The process of doing a literature review involves Poetic Inquiry as 'written from or in response to works of literature/theory in a discipline or field. Or, alternately, these may be poems about poetry and/or inquiry itself' (Prendergast 2009, p. xxii). 'Papers' was written in response to reading a multitude of research papers and concepts during my Ph.D.. In an effort to become a better researcher and strive to better relay concepts and experience in a meaningful and clearer way, the practice of poetry as literature review could provide such insights (Luce-Kapler 2009). Also, Richardson (1997, p. 180) suggests that

> If the goal of ethnography is to retell 'lived experience,' to make another world
> accessible to the reader, then, I submit that the lyric poem, and particularly a sequence
> of lyric poems with an implied narrative, comes closer to achieving that goal than
> other forms of ethnographic writing

Phenomenologically speaking, as poet-researchers we aim to 'Breathe-in experience, breathe-out poetry' (Muriel Rukeyser 1982). Pelias' (2016) work captures this approach in *Leaning*. In particular, he includes a section on 'poeticizing theory' as a tribute to Laurel Richardson's work and response 'to her call for and use of the poetic in sociological and ethnographic research' (p. 79). Similarly, I too, aim to 'pull you in' to the complex and intricate world of a qualitative researcher via my own search for understanding via poetry as literature review or as Pelias calls it 'poeticizing theory'. Pelias (2016) suggests we learn 'into gather lessons that might be learned' (p. 227) and offers those concerned with promoting growth and healing a way of being with poetry. His chapter 'Walking and writing with Laurel Richardson' is a particularly interesting and thought-provoking read that demonstrates how we might 'walk with' people as 'embodied, self-consciously reflexive, partial knowers, conveners, ministers, - not "insiders" or "outsiders"' (Richardson 1997, p. 185). Like Pelias (2016), I want others to respond to my poetry: 'Tell me your stories. Share with me the poetry that makes your life speak. Do not be afraid. I will do my best to honor what you say. We are all flawed, human. Show me how we might connect' (p. 228). When I first read his book, I imagined myself leaning in offering my own stories and poems (Owton, 2014), and now I am doing/writing what I imagined. Similarly to Pelias (2016), I wanted to capture something of the qualitative journey that includes a history of the so-called paradigm wars of the 1980s (Denzin, 2009).

The Long hard wait

If you venture down this rough road,
Be aware! You should be told,
Requirement for being tough – No, not tough. Brave and bold.

A message to other emergin youths,
As I myself ask, '*Am I strong enough?*'
For this unearthin of 'unsettling truths'

What's more, this messy multiplicity threatens the security
in the Scientific community
of their accurately certain Objective reality.

Insecurities fuel taunts of unworthiness,
Attempts to suppress expressiveness,
Kindness mistaken for weakness,
Subjected to ridicule from openness.

'*It's just words innit?*'
'Just writin about yourself innit?'
Bullies exposed as stupid cowards; ignorance to understand
… *is* more like it!

Tough messages to the next generation,
"Build your walls, fuckers! We'll just climb right over them!"
Inter-connected communities embrace; relief from dominating con-
frontation.

"What is it about? What is NOT said? What is challenged?"
Is this falling on inexperienced duped ears deafened by the dominat-
ing?
Criticised for self-indulgence is intellectually insulting,
Self-exposed needs acceptance… still fucking waiting!

Others might identify with some of the difficulties, challenges and conversations associated with qualitative research in this poem. I employ another example that can be broken down a bit more and explored. I draw on the concept known as 'The Imposter phenomena' to demonstrate what I mean, here, in more detail. The imposter phenomena is common in academia and was initially termed by Pauline Rose Clance and Suzanne Imes in 1978 used to 'designate an internal experience of intellectual phonies' (p. 1). Clance and Imes were psychotherapists and worked with over 150 highly successful women. Despite being recognised for their academic excellence or highly respected in their professional fields, they seemed to consider themselves as 'imposters'. This imposter phenomena is particularly prevalent in high-achieving women (Clance and Imes 1978; Watson 2013), but high-achieving men (Hanks, 2016) have also reported experiencing the phenomena. Since 1978, research suggests the phenomena are much more widely spread than originality thought with it being found to affect 70% of the global population (Clark et al. 2014) although such figures are subject to scrutiny. For women, Clance and Imes (1978) suggest that early family dynamics and later introjection of societal sex-role stereotyping can contribute significantly to the development of the phenomena. Indeed, Clance and Imes (1978, p. 1) go further to suggest that

> women who experience the imposter phenomenon persists in believing that they are really not bright and have fooled anyone who thinks otherwise. Numerous achievements, which one might expect to provide ample object evidence of superior intellectual functioning, do not appear to affect the impostor belief.

To understand my position relative to these phenomena, I decided to write a poem about it which involved positioning myself in amongst the feelings and thoughts associated with being an imposter. In a way, the process of writing poetry as literature review is similar to writing a poem from transcribed verbatim. To capture the essence of this concept, some of the terminology needs to be included and some of the phrases associated with feeling like an imposter. Also, I wanted to make light of this phenomena given how widespread it is and use it as an attempt to help others to recognise that they are not alone in their fears of being 'found out'. The poem is called 'Getting away with it'.

Getting away with it

Sometimes…
I have all this nagging self-doubt,
I secretly worry,
I have fears horrendously,
That everyone'll find out,
"I'm really not as bright as you think I am"
It's all a scam

Despite various:
~ Reviews, potential publications,
~ Poetic representations,
~ Presentations…
I *still* seem to think,
"Phew, fooled 'em!"
"Fluke wasn't it"
I'm always on the brink,
Just waiting,
waiting
waiting
One day someone will realise I'm not so clever,
They'll kick me out,
The illusion will crumble,
"*Get out you imposter!*

I would happily admit,
unmask my fraudulent reputation,
accept failed expectations,
"I knew it!"

not yet

People just seem to like me,
I think that's why I get away with it!

Lynda Moore (1986) suggests that writing therapy can be a helpful activity because it attempts to alleviate a person's sense of inadequacy that is often experienced with the imposter phenomena. There are various other methods for addressing the imposter phenomena but writing therapy can help (re)organise a person's thoughts and feelings (Pennebaker 2010). Therefore, poetry could not only be a way to understand a particular phenomenon or theory but also address feelings of inadequacy. I discuss poetry as therapy in Chap. 6 in more detail.

Another example I draw from is about the researcher's responsibility in current times of academia. During my Ph.D., I faced the dilemmas many researchers might experience; I explored how I managed boundaries within research encounters (Owton and Allen-Collinson 2014). I employed vignettes to explore potential issues and confusion that can arise from being friends with or related to participants, and how this can blur the ethical boundaries. At times, I felt quite a responsibility when I had to decide what these multiple roles involved and how to maintain each equally, particularly with the potential for significant consequences in relation to my research, my friendships and family relationships. These issues can be even more magnified when investigating more sensitive topics, such as sexual abuse in sport (see Owton 2016). In light of the changing academic environment, I wrote a poem called Author's responsibility in an attempt to capture and reflect the issues involved in negotiating the author's positioning and moral sense of duty and responsibility when writing up research.

Author's responsibility

Moral obligation for faithful legitimacy; questionability,
Does this only serve my own selfish needs?
Is it genuine authenticity?
Reflectively taking authority,
Out of respect for my friendly,
Ever helpful participants for their contribution,
Wanting to educate others with their story,
Caught amidst the dilemmas of governmental stipulation,
Blue skies replaced with impact factor, prestige journals,
To have to build a 'high-status' reputation,
Reductionist values reduce sincere satisfaction,
But then, returning
Accepting author responsibility,
Returning reciprocity, unfinalizing empathy,
Keeping an honest respectable ethical attitude for them and for me.

Kim Etherington (2004) recognises that as we enter into relationships with participants then we must face issues of power that accompany researchers when we write about other people's lives. This requires us 'constantly to scrutinize and interrogate our own positions, views, and behaviours, turning back onto ourselves the same scrupulous lens through which we examine the lives of our participants' (p. 226). Etherington (2004) and Josselson (1996) argue that power can make us feel uncomfortable but if we recognise and accept that power, along with the feelings of anxiety that might accompany that power, then we can become more aware of the ethical issues and monitor them and our feelings as the research unfolds. Whilst writing about others can give rise to addressing ethical concerns, complexities, tensions and conflicts, writing about the reflexive process can be accompanied by greater concerns;

how our participants might feel when they read our reflexive stories; the risks involved with academic criticism; and how much or how little to disclose about ourselves as researchers (Etherington 2004). The chapter that follows discusses some of these concerns in more depth and considers employing poetry as a form of reflective writing. Before I move on to the next chapter, however, poetry as literature review can take a political focus.

Politicising Poetry

Whilst we might talk about poeticising theory, we might also think about politicising poetry although arguably the 'personal is political' when referring to power relationships (Hanisch, 2006). Whilst there is a debate that poetry and politics are not always intertwined, some poets have employed poetry as a way to fight political battles. Similarly to musicians writing politically (e.g. Grace Petrie), Benjamin Zephaniah is well known for his poetry and politics; employing poetry to make a difference to society. He argues that 'you kind of knock people out with the politics. Sometimes you can make people aware of the situation if you show them the absurdity of it and get them to laugh at it' (Zephaniah 2012, para 8). Inspired by Zephaniah's poems, an example I wish to include here is written in response to stories I read about violence against women.

To the victims

Hey you, please don't think we don't *feel* your pain
your frustration, your anger must *feel* so raw
We *feel* the world going insane!
We can imagine this must just *feel* like the last straw

Hey you, please don't think that we don't believe you
Just when you thought you had justice on your side
The bastard came back to re-traumatise you through and through
Bribery disgrace; it must *feel* like all hope has died.

Hey you, *We* believe you, don't give up hope
We must carry on fighting against the miscarriage of justice
Violence against women is no joke; a serious crime to have to cope
with alone. *We* feel so much disgust.

We know what happened to you was very real, unfair
Blurry realisations of abuse uncovered
Remember, the best revenge is to *care*
about yourself. A new life will be discovered.

References

Clance, P. R., & Imes, S. A. (1978). The imposter phenomenon in high achieving women: Dynamics and therapeutic intervention. *Psychotherapy: Theory Research and Practice, 15*(3), 241–247.

Clark, M., Vardeman, K., & Barba, S. (2014). Perceived inadequacy: A study of the imposter phenomenon among college and research librarians. *College & Research Libraries, 75*(3), 255–271.

Denzin, N. (2009). *Qualitative inquiry under fire: Toward a new paradigmdialogue*. Walnut Creek, CA: Left Coast Press.

Etherington, K. (2004). *Becoming a reflexive researcher*. London: Jessica Kingsley.

Hanisch, C. (2006). The Personal Is Political: The Women's Liberation Movement classic with a new explanatory introduction. Available: http://www.carolhanisch.org/CHwritings/PIP.html. Accessed 19 April 2017.

Josselson, R. (1996). *Ethics and process in the narrative study of lives* (Vol. 4). London: Sage.

Luce-Kapler, R. (2009). Serendipity, poetry and inquiry. In M. Prendergast, C. Leggo, and P. Sameshima, P. (Eds.), *Poetic inquiry: Vibrant voices in the social sciences* (pp. 75–78). Rotterdam: Sense Publishers.

Moore, Lynda L. (1986). *Not as far as you think: The realities of working women*. Lexington, MA.: Lexington Books.

Owton, H. (2014). Leaning: A Poetics of Personal Relations. *Journal of Poetry Therapy, 27*(3), 157–160.

Owton, H. (2016). *A qualitative case study of sexual abuse in sport* (p. 109). Basingstoke: Palgrave. Publishers. ISBN 978-3319467955.

Owton, H., & Allen-Collinson, J. (2014). Close but not too close: Friendship as method (ology) in ethnographic research encounters. *Journal of Contemporary Ethnography, 43*(3), 283–305.

Pelias, R. J. (2016). *Leaning: A poetics of personal relations*. London: Routledge.

Pennebaker, J. W. (2010). Expressive writing in a clinical setting. *The Independent Practitioner, 30*, 23–25.

Prendergast, M. (2009). Introduction: The phenomena of poetry in research: "Poem is what?" Poetic inquiry in qualitative social science research. In M. Prendergast, C. Leggo, and P. Sameshima, P. (Eds.), *Poetic inquiry: Vibrant voices in the social sciences* (pp. 13–29).

Richardson, L. (1997). *Fields of play: Constructing an academic life*. New Brunswick: Rutgers University Press.

Rukeyser, M. (1982). Poem out of childhood. In M. Prendergast, C. Leggo, and P. Sameshima, P. (Eds.), *Poetic inquiry: The collected poems of Muriel Rukeyser* (p. 3). New York: McGraw-Hill.

Watson, E. (2013). I suffered from imposter syndrome after Harry Potter. *Now Magazine*, Available: http://www.celebsnow.co.uk/celebrity-news/emma-watson-i-suffered-from-imposter-syndrome-after-harry-potter-i-felt-like-a-fraud-90219.

Zephaniah, B. (2012). Benjamin Zephaniah: There isn't enough anger in politics. *The Guardian*, Available: https://www.theguardian.com/books/2012/dec/28/benjamin-zephaniah-anger-politics-interview. Accessed 19 April 2017.

CHAPTER 6

Poetry as Reflective Writing

Abstract As noted earlier in some of the debates surrounding Poetic Inquiry, one might ask: *What qualifies you to conduct Poetic Inquiry?* This section considers the debated concept of poetry as therapy amidst the importance of self-care of the researcher. Poetry is a risky business, and qualitative researchers in general have to always 'prove' themselves (Cahnmann-Taylor 2009). Researchers, such as Butler-Kisber and Stewart (in: Prendergast et al. (eds). Poetic inquiry, Sense publishers, Boston, 2009), highlight discussions about the professional practices of those who employ poetry as a tool of inquiry and urge them to read more poetry, take creative writing classes, and take more risks in our field notes and articles. This section provides some examples along with some tasks on how to write reflectively (e.g. writing experiments to encourage a 'stream of consciousness').

Keywords Reflectivity · Writing · Therapy · Emotion

Reflexivity

Reflexivity is 'an ability to notice our responses to the world around us, other people and events, and use that to inform our actions, communications and understandings' (Etherington 2004, p. 19). Reflexivity is an important aspect of professional practice, in research and of intellectual

H. Owton, *Doing Poetic Inquiry*, Palgrave Studies in Creativity and Culture, DOI 10.1007/978-3-319-64577-3_6

work, and even as I write this book I am constantly shifting in my multi-layered understanding of the world. Reflexivity requires more than self-awareness; it is a dynamic process requiring a conversation about experience whilst simultaneously living in the moment (Etherington 2004). Writing reflectively might allow one to step outside one's own experience and view it with fresh, renewed and open eyes. Reflexive practice enables us to reflect on life and to find shape in meanings. Given the role of the poet in research, it is important to understand our hearts, our inner story and how we are active agents in the process. Reflexivity encourages researchers to be meticulous, reflective and open-minded with a critical approach (Silverman 2000). Given the emotional maturity and strong interpersonal skills required in qualitative research to collect data or, more precisely, hear the stories of others and use their words to describe phenomena (Collins and Cooper 2014), one can become a better researcher by writing reflexively. Specifically, Luce-Kapler (2009) argues that writing poetry enables one to endeavour to convey experience to an audience in a meaningful way where unanticipated insights can occur.

When I write poetry, sometimes it feels like I am driven by a strong but blurred peripheral force where my body seems to be engaged in both an outward projection to the world, to the environment, and a falling back receding into unknown visceral depths as a way to gain self-understanding (Leder 1990). In Leder's (1990) understanding, the body is no longer 'absent' by virtue of disappearance and through body-focusing, 'we experience from the body to something outside' (Duesund and Skårderud 2003, p. 59). When responding to writing, if it is done well, listeners respond emotionally—they *feel something* as a result of the story which 'brings a certain degree of physical involvement to the listener/reader' (Douglas and Carless 2009, p. 317). Burns (2003) argues that working viscerally and deeply means that readers may identify with the stories; they may learn from them or they may find them irrelevant. Working viscerally, Burns (2003) argues that we are more likely to be 'drawn into it because something there speaks to our deeper selves, gets inside us and takes hold' (p. 1).

Researchers can write reflexivity to enhance an understanding of the self (Carless 2012; Douglas 2009; Etherington 2004), and this can be done via poetry (Gilbourne 2011). As McAdams (1993, p. 11) states:

> If you want to know me, then you must know my story, for my story defines who I am. And if I want to know myself, to gain insight into the meaning of my own life, then I, too, must come to know my own story.

Furthermore, writing doesn't seem to be *just* writing—writing involves being reflexive.

It is a dynamic creative and unearthing practice which can be a method of analysis and subjected to interpretation (Richardson 2000). It is worth noting the risks involved in reflecting *too* much and finding oneself going round in circles and achieving very little—like a hamster whizzing round in a wheel. Since poetry is also an art form, crafting a poem is a process and it may never feel finished but as Griffin (1995) reminds us, the poem *is* the thing which is located in a complex space and time (Leggo 2008). Therefore, the selected poems below which I wrote during my Ph.D. are completed because of some *felt* finalisation whilst maintaining the meanings, through the crafting of poetry.

Acquiring a doctorate is a key milestone in becoming an independent researcher. Much of the discourse surrounding doctorate education focuses on the 'autonomous self' (Pilbeam and Denyer 2009). Indeed, doctoral study is deemed to epitomise independent learning. However, whilst independence does not necessarily mean that an individual needs to be isolated, studying a Ph.D. can be accompanied with intense loneliness and isolation. As a doctoral student, there is also a desire to be accepted into the academic field. This desire has been a source of anxiety for some young academics who strive to 'fit in' (see Archer 2008). For these reasons, doctorate students can experience a roller coaster of emotions in isolation during their studies. Furthermore, as a qualitative researcher, there is the need to come to terms with the personal uneasiness and uncertainty of locating one's self in the midst of their research and participants in their study. Thus, unsettling feelings can be further magnified during this type of doctorate. In such a situation, commensurate with a phenomenologically inspired approach, writing from the body can mean seeing with one's own eyes rather than seeing the representation constructed by the eyes of another, which could be a beneficial self-help strategy (Cubbison 1997).

Expressive writing of poetry was adopted as a way to cope and reflect on past experiences through the first year of Chan's (2003) Ph.D. A range of poems were written during an insight into higher education, qualitative research and self-reflection. I experienced a complexity of emotions which were important to acknowledge as a source of increasing self-understanding. A saying often heard is: 'it's better out than in'; there are ducts other than tears (Bolton 1999), and expressive writing was used as a catharsis in my first year. Indeed, as Wright and Chung (2001) point out 'the pen is more powerful than the pill' (p. 283). Some of the poems below capture these moments.

Unearthing the rug

There's this rug in this house; forgotten presence,
Cornered; wrapped in unsettling 'webs of significance'.

Feelings of resentment lean towards the uselessness of this rug,
Forgetting how angrily you rage against its fate!
Knocking it, falling occasionally, bumping like a thug.
Remembering then… —this repulsive rug twisted in denial—you hate!

Ambivalence emanates towards revolting resistance,
Convenient excuses, weighted dreaded heaviness,
Unavoidable 'fitting' distractions; laziness,
Aggravating thoughts of disturbance.

Fears to unravel the repulsive rug; disquieting mess and disgusting creeps,
Nested dirt and slime inside; ignorance is your refuge… unfairness deeply seeps.
Anything could be hidden taped in the deepest darkest corners,
Curious compassionate souls continuously enquire about it.
It's been ignored, left, sat there stewing for *so* long now,
Perhaps shreds of rotting bitterness already simmers.

Time to sort this nagging old rug out; tensioned awkward relatedness…
slowly unfolding… bit…by…bit.
Adapting contextual horrors… perceptual courage! Need to be wholly fit.
Sincerely, beginning sobering trudge.

Part of the process of becoming a qualitative researcher can be painful as it requires a researcher to reflect on their pasts, memories, experiences, emotions and position in the research (Etherington 2004). The process of writing messy data can give rise to difficult emotions as a qualitative researcher. As Krane (2016, p. 473) notes, 'too often it is swept under the rug and disregarded as an intentional process when describing our analytical procedure'. Whilst reflexivity and management strategies involve enhancing trustworthiness, authenticity and credibility of the research (Creswell 2009), also, writing reflexively in a journal can be a helpful self-care strategy. Many recognise the emotional risks involved in research, particularly when working with sensitive issues (e.g. Owton 2016; Owton and Allen-Collinson 2017; Owton and Sparkes 2017). Brackenridge (1999) discusses strategies for personal survival as a researcher investigating sensitive issues serving to emphasise the importance of researcher 'self-care'. She proposed a 'self-management framework' involving coping with stress, coping with being alone and privileging the personal, political or scientific self. I am not alone when I say that I believe that it is important for researchers to take part in self-care strategies and develop support from network circles in your own fields of research. Increasingly, more generally, the value of making time for self-care is becoming well recognised in different professions. In medical professions, Hatem and Ferrera (2001) and Shapiro and Rucker (2003) argue that creative writing may aid in the professional development of medical practitioners (e.g. medical doctors and physicians). Poetry is just one form of writing that could have therapeutic and cathartic effects.

Poetry as Therapy

Human expression has been described as being 'the heart of human perception' (Eigen 1986, p. 291). Creative writing can be a way of expressing our perceptions, as well as our feelings, thoughts, reflections and emotions. The therapeutic and developmental power of expressive creative writing has been explored by researchers (e.g. Bolton 1999) in Medical humanities over the last 20 years. Whilst art therapies have been available to Britain for quite some time, writing, specifically, poetry is still emerging as a recognised therapy or as a valuable reflective tool. Historically, humans have expressed their emotions through music. Similarly, poetry is also a means of sublimating aggressive, amorous or perhaps radical impulses. Some write with love and elation, some in agony, angst and frustration, or with seething rage. Feelings of anger could be alleviated, particularly when writing with rage because writing could act as a catharsis, providing relief or therapy. This can sometimes be noticed in the rhythm of the poem where vitalising impulses transforms accumulated violence into creative discharge. Either way, the process of creative writing can be exciting and enjoyable and can also increase and/or build confidence and self-respect (Bolton 1999). To add to additional debates about whether poetry is data or an *art* form in Poetic Inquiry, research as some form of therapy can be frowned upon, but it is very common for people to use poetry as a form of healing; it can be used as a way of trying to let go of the past.

Letting go

Difficulty not staring when one door closes,
Grieving allowance,
Untying hands from past entrapment,
Slowly searching for another door; openness.

Don't have to give up to let go,
Don't have to totally lose control,
Playful; go with the flow.

New life; new self accept,
Changing meanings; old historical concepts,
Learning alternative perspectives,
Unthreatening; not manipulative,
Different ways of being responsive,
Thinking; not always reacting sharpish.

Don't have to give up to let go,
Don't have to totally lose control,
Playful; go with the flow.

Bolton (1999) points out that poetry and medicine have gone hand in hand since the time of the Ancient Greeks. Greeks recognised the healing power of poetry (Hitchings 1969). Poets have revealed and analysed the human condition long before the study of human behaviour was conceptualised as a science (Hitchings 1969). It is surprising then, that poetry therapy in the UK is not as widely acknowledged or established as it is in the USA. The National Association for Poetry Therapy in the USA represents one of the most developed of the creative writing therapies. In the UK, there is slow development with The Association for the Literary Arts in Personal Development (LAPIDUS) which focuses on 'creative writing'. Nonetheless, it is becoming more recognised as a therapy with Bolton's (1999) research primarily challenging the British medical profession to undertake a new, creative way of working with patients. She stresses the power of writing in a setting where patients are all too often passive and powerless. Indeed, too much medicine is diagnosis from the outside and having treatments inflicted onto the patient (Bolton 1999). With poetry writing, many people are able to guide their own therapy because writing in itself is a very powerful technique (Wright and Chung 2001). It has been found by other researchers (e.g. Lerner and Bettinger 1991) that poetic writing can be considered a clinical means to self-understanding. Furthermore, poetry writing has been recognised as a self-help strategy for coping with stress (Greenhaigh 1999), and it has even been found that those with chronic illnesses who write about the most stressful experiences can lead to improvement in disease severity (Smyth et al. 1999). It is not clearly known why poetry is effective in bringing about physical changes in health and behaviour change (Esterling et al. 1999).

Shapiro and Stein (2005) considered the possibility that poetry acted as a healing influence on medical students as a way to make emotional sense about the different relationships they encounter during their training. Additionally, power can be felt in the voicing of yourself through poetry. It can be a very valuable process when someone finds it more difficult to talk about their problems than to write about them. Indeed, Fox (1997, p. 3) describes the therapeutic value of poetry:

> Poetry helps us feel our lives rather than be numb. The page, touched with our poem, becomes a place for painful feelings to be held, explored and transformed. Writing and reading poems is a way of naming where we have been, where we are, and where we are going in our lives.

As mentioned in an earlier chapter, Chan (2003) found that her Ph.D. was a traumatic event in her life and in the event of disruption, poetry may help to create order where chaos existed, whether the chaos is the individual or in his/her relationship with others (Berger 1969). This is perhaps because creative writing, particularly poetry, helps to reflect back, to constructively reminisce, to recollect and reintegrate one's present self with one's past selves, and gain a sense of wholeness and fullness of life (Bolton 1999). In this sense, poetry may be used to reflect inner turbulent experiences and thus the inner becomes the outer (or the conscious), making it tangible and workable (Hitchings 1969). Therefore, poetry writing can profoundly alter the writer, similarly to a researcher undertaking qualitative research, because the process faces one with oneself (Bolton 1999).

In Chap. 1, I refer to a poem I wrote about my father and writing as reflective practice has been a helpful process for me to foster connections with myself, the past, the present and others, and be open to the idea and beauty of uncertainty in the process of healing. Like Leggo (2008), I want to 'live poetically, and that means living emotionally with my feelings in motion and commotion' (p. 168). Drawing you back to the first chapter where I wrote about my father, I have rewritten about my father at various points in my life (Owton 2012) which demonstrates the multifaceted nature of analysing poetry located in a complex space and time.

20 Years Later…

Spreading the world with what you left me,
In a squeezed time-frame,
All the proverbs on your office cupboard door,
Kept treasured; enveloped in my memory,
Opening when opportunities face me.

Eyes smiling; you live through us,
Paying lip service; my spiritual reliance,
Working all the hours; sacrificial consequence,
Family business importance,
Windsurfing was your escape; always trying to balance,

"Sitting on the dock of the bay"
Taking opportune moments.

Not a man of many words,
That's what people say,
and what I remember,
Only if things were absurd!
Recession attacked your heart!
For educational significance.

"Oooo, that's why I'm easy,
I'm easy like Sunday morning"

It's not always easy…
because you're *not* here and you still *died* Daddy.

Faultless; in my heart
Gazing at the stars,
still feeling your presence anyway.

As previously noted, Griffin (1995, p. 191) points out, 'poetry does not describe. It *is* the thing. It is an experience, not the secondhand record of an experience, but the experience itself' and Leggo reminds us that 'the poet always understands that she or he is located in a complex space and time' (p. 167). Through this understanding, poet-researchers do not conduct interviews or gather data to determine whether the meaning expressed actually corresponds to events that have really occurred. This is in line with interpretive ontological beliefs when conducting qualitative research. The poet-researcher does not view the research encounter as a 'conquest' (Ezzy 2010). The 'truth', sought by many poet-researchers then, is 'poetic truths', or 'narrative truths' not 'historical' truths.

Similarly to dream analysis, there is an opportunity to delve into the mind of the poet by sifting through the maze of phrases, metaphors, images and symbols (Bolton 1999). Some suggest (Wright and Chung, 2001) that there is a theoretical need to combine and to work across disciplines in the field of writing therapy (drawing on psychoanalytic theory, linguistics, symbolic interactionism and philosophy, ancient and modern). Expressive writing enriched my perspective, self-expression, reduced anxiety and loneliness, enabled me to articulate written communication from the unconscious, a meaningful understanding of new insights, and felt a sense of deepening healing. Poetry as expressive writing has sometimes acted as a self-help alternative healing process. Indeed, the use of poetry is a phenomenology access point to the world by allowing people to find their own unique voice (DeMaria 1991). Writing poetry is a way of grasping life, nurturing every bit of good, connecting up severed bits of ourselves; it is written from our whole self—mind, spirit and body. Through creative work, one can come to see, at a glance, a certain rhythmic flow in mood, the ups and downs, high-lows related to different phases in one's efforts (Bassin et al. 1986). 'Poetry, even when it concerns death, pain disfigurement, despair, is vibrant, alive, a way of life' (Bolton 1999, p. 130).

As qualitative researchers, we might find ourselves working with participants who might engage in poetry as healing, also. Douglas and Carless (2012) discuss the issues concerning researcher–participant relationships and highlight how reciprocity, supportiveness and care are critical. Here, I provide a powerful, empathetic and evocative example from Bella, a participant engaged in research on sexual abuse in sport, using poetry as therapy.

Having a chat

I think it's about time we had a chat,
Cos I really *feel* your pain
                                        your fear,
Realities undone,
                        blurred; unclear,
You need to realise, what happened was unfair,
You need to realise, what you feel;
                                        it was very real; *care!*

Hey kid, you lost your Daddy; not his fault,
Your Mummy broke down; emotional jolt,
A target! You needed attention,
Care! Not groomed abuse, assault, or neglection.

All this terminological realisation!

Now… you *are* safer,
                                        You don't have to suffer
                                                    in isolation,
Punishment; self blame,
                                        inflict self-harming behaviour,
Fear of abandonment, rejection,
Take your finger off that button,
Don't spiral into self destruction.

No need to sleep with your clothes on,
Suck your thumb; hide in your room,
At night, leave on the light,
Roam the dark streets; drinking into oblivion,
Feeling all numb or all uptight…

What happened to you was very real,

Traumatic; it's hard not to feel
scared.
Sensing danger; remember…
The worst is over.
I *know* you; I *feel* your pain,
Your racing heart; I *feel* your fear,
I *believe* you; you're *not* going insane!

Thanks for opening up to me,
For being honest,
It's up to me; I can now see,
I'm here; I'll do my best,
I'm strong! *As* tough as you,
You *really* don't need to worry.

Your puppet strings were cut loose,
We'll build strength; do what we choose
to make us better.
Hey kid, don't get manic!
Feel your body; stroke your hands, stamp your feet,
Look around the room; B r e e e a a a t h e
slow, DEEP.
Creating boundaries; trusting people…
We'll hold you; talking, touching, reminding,
In the *now* feeling,
when you start to panic,
Won't feel so terrible.

We'll break this spiralling chain,
We can do it,
together. Start anew,
I'll *always* be here looking after you…
being *kind* to you,
loving you; just trust me a bit,
Protected; no harm will *ever*
come to you *ever* again,
we'll make sure of it.

How to Write Reflectively

Some people find writing poetry intimidating; poetry itself can come with a loaded sense of elitism. There are different ways to write reflectively (e.g. writing a letter, writing a story and writing streams of consciousness), and poetry is just another form of writing which allows you to think deeply or carefully about something. Writing allows emotions and thinking to connect which is what Goleman terms 'emotional intelligence' (1996) and as 'social intelligence' (2006). According to this logic, there is some evidence to suggest that emotionally aware children are more successful in exams and at work, have happier marriages and lead healthier lives. In a culture which seems to devalue emotions, it can be difficult to integrate emotions and thinking together. To begin, however, there are some exercises that might help you to start writing poetically and reflectively.

You might start a poem with the following phrases:

- 'I am thinking…' (write down what you are thinking at the moment)
- 'I am feeling…' (explore different emotions and write down where you feel that emotion in your body)
- 'I can see… I can hear… I can smell… I can taste…' (notice the things around you in that moment)
- 'I am thinking…' (write down what you are thinking at that very moment)
- 'I would like to thank you for…' (treat this poem like you are writing a thank you letter to someone)
- 'I want to tell you a story about…' (use this poem as a narrative to shape a story)
- 'My ideal day…' (use this poem as a way to imagine a perfect day)
- 'The concept of… is like…' (use this poem to describe a theory or a concept)
- 'My dog is like…' (sometimes we can gain great insight about ourselves when we describe our pets)

At this stage, do not worry about rhyming and let the rhythm take its natural beat but think about how you might change what you are feeling and notice what sorts of observations and thoughts might be accompanied by different feelings. You might notice that you choose to observe, hear, sense or pay attention to certain things. Also, think about considering and including the following:

- Emotions
- Metaphors
- Images and descriptions
- Smells
- Tastes
- Sounds
- Colour
- People, wildlife, animals
- Texture
- Judgement
- Opinion
- Internal dialogue.

Once you have made a start, you can think about crafting your words and thinking about stanza length and other techniques. Remember that no first draft is perfect; I'm sure nobody ever saw or commented on Einstein's first draft. No writer really creates a good first draft and regardless of what others tell you it is hard work, and writing and poetry take time—poetry cannot be done in haste and why would you want to rush it? I have overheard science students criticise another student for submitting a poem, saying how easy it must have been but that's simply not true. Writing takes practice and reflexive practice takes time and can be challenging, stimulating and enlightening. I believe it can make us much more thoughtful, insightful, intellectual, kind and empathetic practitioners and researchers. Phenomenologically inspired writing requires writing from the body and writing with emotion.

Writing from the Body

Writing is physical, creating a tangible resource; 'the movement of the pen/cil over the page, and the contemplation of the product, can give pleasure and satisfaction' (Bolton 1999, p. 120). Bolton recognises that whilst writing is a satisfying physical creative process, 'the writing hand not only seems to know what the thinking mind does, but also knows how much that mind, as well as the feeling heart, can bear to face' (Bolton 1999, p. 121). Similarly, to Cubbison (1997), writing from the body means that I must write out of a recognition of who I am. The embodied self of the researcher has become recognised as a crucial component of the research process (Allen-Collinson and Hockey 2005; Sparkes 2009). Therefore, writing in isolation means that there is an opportunity to turn inward to the study of one's own self, body, mind and soul combined. It means a way of seeing with one's own perceptivity rather than seeing the representation constructed by the eyes of another (Cubbison 1997).

> I sit. I look intently at the white clean page. I feel the pen between my fingers. I rest the edge of my hand on the surface of the paper. I slowly become immersed in a sensory experience losing sight of the pen, my hand and the page. Gradually my energy awakens, as intangible thoughts, images and fuzzy feelings come into consciousness. My body soon finds rhythm that harmonises my writing with feelings and sense making. I literally lose myself in the poem experiencing a sense of timelessness. Initially, the words are disjointed and nonsensical. Suddenly, the unpredictable becomes an open door to something insightful, new and exciting. I feel a spark inside enlightened from mastery and revelation. Yet… this is not always the way. Sometimes I have to find a different perspective. Stubbornly, avoiding premature closure, I will not settle for an easy solution. I alternate perspectives, shifting in and out of varying cognitive and physical states: getting lost in my work – stepping back and taking perspective. With the emergence of the sensation, the imagery and the meaning inherent in the language taking form, comes a new insight and understanding. It has released realisation and intensity. I feel a sense of conviction. A very personal piece of writing materialises (Owton, diary extract 2010).

Writing from the body means writing without thinking and allowing one's hand to take over: thinking can inhibit this kind of therapeutic writing (Bolton 1999). A sense of shame and humiliation is hard to shift, and it is easier to remain silent than to spend the time and energy talking about things, particularly in an academic environment which encourages an unemotional and impersonal world. However, writing poetry can break silences that need to be overcome in the process of conducting qualitative research. Similarly to forming narratives, poetic narratives can be formed which can help mend psychological processes in self-identity, memory and making meaning. This cannot happen without writing with emotion as well.

Writing with Emotion

Despite the encouragement of emotional detachment in academia, the research process, as I have continuously discovered throughout my research experiences, is not an emotion-free experience. Contrary to this belief, impersonal academic sculpt, effective use of emotions enables individuals to control their instinctive reactions to stressful conditions, to learn to better communicate one's emotional state, to develop healthy relationships, increase empathy levels and become successful in education, work and life (Elias and Weissberg 2000; Gore 2000; Ulutaş and Ömeroğlu 2007). Moreover, Irwin (2006) argues that remaining distant, unemotional and objective can have tragic implications. Previous academic and sporting environments had disciplined and trained me, leading me to a belief that researchers need to be objective and 'extract out' emotion—I had learnt to 'suffer in silence' and used my body as a means of expression through martial arts. Poetry was a step towards breaking that silence of these cultures embedded in my body. Whilst poetry as therapy might not be subjected to analysis and can be used for the sake of healing, in the next chapter, I explore how we can subject poems to judgment.

References

Allen-Collinson, J., & Hockey, J. (2005). Autoethnography: Self-indulgence or rigorous methodology? In M. McNamee (Ed.), *Philosophy and the sciences of exercise, health and sport: Critical perspectives on research methods* (pp. 187–202). London: Routledge.

Archer, L. (2008). The impossibility of minority ethnic educational 'success'? An examination of the discourses of teachers and pupils in British secondary schools. *European Educational Research Journal, 7*(1), 89–107.

Bassin, D., Lyshak, F., & Robbins, A. (1986). The creative act as a means of overcoming resistance in treatment. In A. Robbins (Ed.), *Expressive therapy: A creative arts approach to depth-oriented treatment* (pp. 43–57). New York: Human Science Press.

Berger, M. (1969). Poetry as therapy—and therapy as poetry. In J. Leedy (Ed.), *Poetry therapy* (pp. 75–87). Pennsylvania: Lippincott Company.

Bolton, G. (1999). Every poem breaks a silence that had to be overcome*: The therapeutic power of poetry writing. *Feminist Review, 62*, 118–133.

Brackenridge, C. (1999). Managing myself: Investigator survival in sensitive research. *International Review for the Sociology of Sport, 34*(4), 399–410.

Burns, M. (2003). Creative writing 101: Show vs. tell. *Colorado Springs Fiction Writer's Group*. Available: http://www.coloradospringsfictionwritersgroup.org/archive/2003-10_article-creative_writing_101-show_versus_tell.pdf. Accessed 28 Nov 2009.

Butler-Kisber, L., & Stewart, M. (2009). The use of poetry clusters in poetic inquiry. In M. Prendergast, C. Leggo, & P. Sameshima (Eds.), *Poetic inquiry* (pp. 3–12). Boston: Sense Publishers.

Cahnmann-Taylor, M. (2009). The craft, practice, and possibility of poetry in educational research. In M. Prendergast, C. Leggo, and P. Sameshima (Eds.). *Poetic inquiry: Vibrant voices in the social sciences* (pp. 13–29). Boston: Sense publishers.

Carless, D. (2012). Negotiating sexuality and masculinity in school sport: an autoethnography. *Sport, Education and Society, 17*(5), 607–625.

Chan, Z. (2003). Poetry writing: A therapeutic means for a social work doctoral student in the process of study. *Journal of Poetry Therapy, 16*(1), 5–17.

Collins, C. S., & Cooper, J. E. (2014). Emotional intelligence and the qualitative researcher. *International Journal of Qualitative Methods, 13*(1), 88–103.

Creswell, J. (2009). *Research design* (3rd ed.). London: Sage.

Cubbison, L. (1997). What does it mean to write from the body? *Women and Language, 20*(1), 31–34.

DeMaria, M. (1991). Poetry and therapeutic factors in group therapy. *Journal of Poetry Therapy, 2*(4), 231–241.

Douglas, K. (2009). Storying my self: Negotiating a relational identity in professional sport. *Qualitative Research in Sport and Exercise, 1*(2), 176–190.

Douglas, K., & Carless, D. (2009). Exploring taboo issues in professional sport through a fictional approach. *Reflective Practice, 10*(3), 311–323.

Douglas, K., and Carless, D. (2012). Taboo tales in elite sport: Relationships, ethics, and witnessing. *Psychology of Women Section Review, 14*(2), 50–56.

Duesund, L., & Skårderud, F. (2003). Use the body and forget the body: Treating anorexia nervosa with adapted physical activity. *Clinical child psychology and psychiatry, 8*(1), 53–72.

Eigen, M. (1986). Expression and meaning. In A. Robbins (Ed.), *Expressive therapy: A creative arts approach to depth-oriented treatment* (pp. 291–312). New York: Human Science Press.

Elias, M. J., & Weissberg, R. P. (2000). Primary prevention: Educational approaches to enhance social and emotional learning. *Journal of School Health, 70*(5), 186–190.

Esterling, B. A., L'Abate, L., Murray, E. J., & Pennebaker, J. W. (1999). Empirical foundations for writing in prevention and psychotherapy: Mental and physical health outcomes. *Clinical Psychology Review, 19*(1), 79–96.

Etherington, K. (2004). *Becoming a reflexive researcher*. London: Jessica Kingsley.

Ezzy, D. (2010). Qualitative interviewing as an embodied emotional performance. *Qualitative Inquiry, 16*(3), 163–170.
Fox, J. (1997). *Poetic medicine: The healing art of poem-making*. New York, NY: Putnam.
Gilbourne, D. (2011). Just in time: A reflective poetic monologue. *Reflective Practice, 12*(1), 27–33.
Goleman, D. (1996). Emot ligence. Why it can matter more than IQ. *Learning, 24*(6), 49–50.
Goleman, D. (2006). The socially intelligent. *Educational Leadership, 64*(1), 76–81.
Gore, S.W. (2000). *Enhancing students emotional intelligence and social adeptness*. ERIC database (ED442572), Saint Xavier University.
Greenhaigh, T. (1999). Writing as therapy: Effects on immune mediated illness need substantiation in independent studies. *British Medical Journal, 319*, 270.
Griffin, S. (1995). *The eros of everyday life: Essays on ecology, gender, and society*. New York: Doubleday.
Hatem, D., & Ferrara, E. (2001). Becoming a doctor: Fostering humane caregivers through creative writing. *Patient Education and Counseling, 45*(1), 13–22.
Hitchings, W. (1969). Poetry, a way to fuller awareness. In J. Leedy (Ed.), *Poetry therapy* (pp. 124–132). Pennsylvania: Lippincott Company.
Irwin, K. (2006). Into the dark heart of ethnography: The lived ethics and inequality of intimate field relationships. *Qualitative Sociology, 29*, 155–175.
Krane, V. (2016). Embracing the messiness of qualitative research: Challenges and opportunities for qualitative researchers in sport and exercise. In B. Smith & A. C. Sparkes (Eds.), *Routledge handbook of qualitative research in sport and exercise*. London: Routledge.
Leder, D. (1990). *The absent body*. Chicago: University of Chicago Press.
Leggo, C. (2008). Astonishing silence. In G. Knowles & A. Cole (Eds.). *Handbook of the arts in qualitative research* (pp. 165–174). Thousand Oaks, CA: Sage.
Lerner, A., & Bettinger, S. (1991). Some semantic considerations in poetry therapy. *A Review of General Semantics, 48*(2), 213–218.
Luce-Kapler, R. (2009). Serendipity, poetry and inquiry. In M. Prendergast, C. Leggo, & P. Sameshima (Eds.). *Poetic inquiry: Vibrant voices in the social sciences* (pp. 75–78). Rotterdam: Sense Publisher.
McAdams, D. (1993). *The stories we live by: Personal myths and the making of the self*. New York: Morrow.
Owton, H. (2010). *Paper, in Secrets of the Heart*. London: United Press Publications.
Owton, H. (2012). Streams of bereavement. *Qualitative Inquiry, 20*, 1–4.

Owton, H. (2016). *A qualitative case study of sexual abuse in sport* (p. 109). Basingstoke: Palgrave Publisher. IBSN 978-3319467955.

Owton, H., & Allen-Collinson, J. (2017). Athlete domestic violence: Contaminating acts and the violation of self-boundaries. In A. Milner & Braddock II, J. H. (Eds.), *Women in sports: Breaking barriers, facing obstacles.* California, USA: ABC-CLIO. IBSN: 1-4408-5124-7.

Owton, H., & Sparkes, A. (2017). Sexual abuse and the grooming process in sport: Bella's story. *Sport, Education and Society.* Available: http://www.tandfonline.com/doi/abs/10.1080/13573322.2015.1063484.

Pilbeam, C., & Denyer, D. (2009). Lone scholar or community member? The role of student networks in doctoral education in a UK management school. *Studies in Higher Education, 34,* 301–318.

Richardson, L. (2000). Writing: A method of inquiry. In N. Denzin & Y. Lincoln (Eds.), *Handbook of qualitative research* (2nd ed., pp. 923–948). London: Sage.

Shapiro, J., & Rucker, L. (2003). Can poetry make better doctors? Teaching the humanities and arts to medicalstudents and residents at the University of California, Irvine, College of Medicine. *Academic Medicine, 78*(10),953–957.

Shapiro, J., & Stein, H. (2005). Poetic license: Writing poetry as a way for medical students to examine their professional relational systems. *Families, Systems, & Health, 23*(3), 278.

Silverman, D. (2000). *Doing qualitative research: A practical handbook.* London: Sage.

Smyth, J. M., Stone, A. A., Hurewitz, A., & Kaell, A. (1999). Effects of writing about stressful experiences on symptom reduction in patients with asthma or rheumatoid arthritis: A randomized trial. *JAMA, 281*(14), 1304–1309.

Sparkes, A. (2009). Ethnography and the senses: challenges and possibilities. *Qualitative Research in Sport and Exercise, 1,* 21–35.

Ulutaş, İ., & Ömeroğlu, E. (2007). The effects of an emotional intelligence education program on the emotional intelligence of children. *Social Behavior and Personality: An International Journal, 35*(10), 1365–1372.

Wright, J., & Chung, M. (2001). Mastery or mystery? Therapeutic writing: A review of the literature. *British Journal of Guidance and Counselling, 29,* 277–291.

CHAPTER 7

Judging Poetic Inquiry

Abstract Qualitative research has taken different turns over the years which has meant a need for a greater understanding of how one might judge new and emerging forms of qualitative research. Instead of taking a criteriology approach, this chapter argues, along with others, that a list of characterising traits (characterising an artful science) needs to be available to reviewers when judging qualitative research.

Keywords Judging qualitative research · Criteriology · Artful science

As more academics question the way of being and way of researching topics in higher education, in ways that attempt to find connection, significance and meaning, some argue for a methodology of the heart. In the words of Pelias (2004, p. 10),

'a heart finds its vocabulary in the senses. It wants a 'sensuous scholarship', 'a mixing of head and heart' (Stoller 2010, xviii). Instead of a 'bloodless prose that saps the body of its sensuousness' (xv), it wants a poem. It wants to be set free.'

It makes sense then to judge Poetic Inquiry on how a poem makes your heart beat, ache, jump, chuckle and listen.

Whilst many argue that this might not be a new approach, there is still a resistance to accept these forms of research from journals. Intense

H. Owton, *Doing Poetic Inquiry*, Palgrave Studies in Creativity and Culture, DOI 10.1007/978-3-319-64577-3_7

debates surround issues of validity in qualitative inquiry. In the traditional positivist definition, validity is the extent to which a test measures what it claims to measure, and it is vital for a test to be valid in order for the results to be accurately applied and interpreted (Jary and Jary 2005). Many scholars (e.g. Dale 1996; Denzin 2009, 2010; Lincoln 1995; Sparkes and Smith 2009) suggest that the traditional criteria (validity, reliability and generalisability) used to evaluate research are inappropriate to apply to research which is underpinned by different philosophical assumptions, and thus requires different judgement criteria more aligned with its naturalistic orientation. Wolcott (1994) talks about the 'absurdity of validity' and argues that he does not accept validity as an appropriate criterion for guiding or judging his research. Sparkes (2001) considers four different perspectives in relation to validity: *replication perspective; parallel perspective; diversification of meanings perspective; letting go perspective*. He suggests that the 'letting go' perspective is where some researchers have chosen to question, or even completely abandon the notion of validity. Given Poetic Inquiry approaches, the concept of validity is similarly problematic. Part of the reason that poetic representations can be risky is precise because they violate a sense of safety and security for those committed to sociological and psychological traditional forms of judgment which abide by questions of validity, reliability and truth (Sparkes and Douglas, 2007; Sparkes and Smith 2009). Poetic representations problematise traditional conceptions of reliability and validity from 'knowing' and 'telling' and bring other more relevant criteria into play for judging the work (Sparkes and Douglas 2007).

Qualitative researchers tend to have to 'prove' themselves, and Poetic Inquiry is often critiqued with regard to issues of validity, reliability and that it is naturally not science. As mentioned earlier, once we realise that the claims to 'scientific truth' are suspect, 'influenced by the culturally bound nature of the researcher's text, we can free ourselves to write in ways that name feeling, story, and relationship' (Cahnmann-Taylor 2009, p. 22). Not only is Poetic Inquiry a risky business because it receives criticism from the traditional positivist scientific paradigm but from the arts. This could be why there are debates around what qualifies someone to conduct Poetic Inquiry. As I explained earlier, my own experience in poetry stems from childhood exposure to poetry, poetry modules when studying English for two years at university, poetry readings and further attendances (and performances) at poetry evenings in the public and academic domain and publications in journals and books. Many researchers (Denzin 2010; Prendergast et al. 2009; Richardson 2000; Sparkes et al. 2003) are confident that alternative, arts-based methods (Leavy 2015) are rigorous, relevant and insightful, and they have taken risks and explored new methods for analysis and publication that experiment at the scientific perimeter to push our questions outward and enhance the field. Drawing on Hugo's (1992) concept of 'triggering towns' and 'obsessive ears', I also argue that if we enhance our ability to notice, name and make sense of regularities and irregularities in the stress patterns of everyday speech in our commonplace settings, we gain a heightened sense of language through the 'art of listening' (Back 2007; Cahnmann-Taylor 2009).

As mentioned previously, many have long argued that it is inappropriate to apply traditional criteria to experimental forms of representation if they are to be given a fair chance to prove their worth. Furthermore, it has been identified that universal criteria are built upon shaky philosophical foundations (Sparkes and Smith 2009). Therefore, different and emerging criteria need to be evoked that call upon multiple sources, including the arts and aesthetics as well as the sciences (see Denzin 2009; Faulkner 2005; Leavy 2015; Sparkes and Smith 2009; Burke 2016). Drawing on characterising traits and debates on how to judge qualitative research, this chapter highlights how we might judge Poetic Inquiry. This does not mean that 'anything goes', quite the contrary! Instead, the open-ended lists of characteristic traits are brought to judgment with the permanent capacity to add items and to subtract items from the lists (Smith and Deemer 2000; Sparkes and Smith 2009). For example, when judging creative analytical practices, perhaps one would consider whether these 'contribute to knowledge', or whether there is a 'comprehensiveness of evidence', or whether it is 'respectful'. These lists are not exhaustive, and I clarify how one might represent the data and be judged by listing characterised traits for specific purposes.

Characterising 'Artful Science'

I draw from Sparkes and Smith (2009) to construct a list of characterised traits. Specifically, Faulkner (2005) blends artistic and scientific concerns from Richardson (2000), Bochner (2000), Clough (2000), Denzin and Lincoln (2011) and Hartnett (2003) to create guidelines for an 'artful science'. Through the conjoining of artistic and scientific criteria she reveals an intersection locating poetic criteria as (Fig. 7.1):

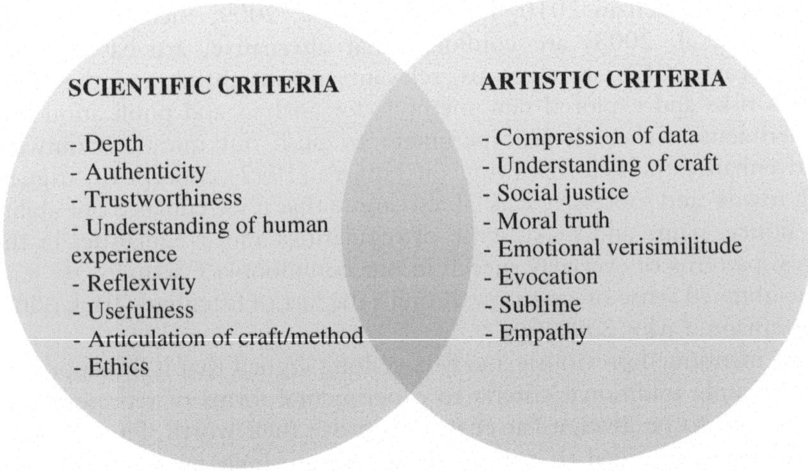

Fig. 7.1 Based on Faulkner's poetic criteria (2005, p. 24)

POETIC TICK LIST

- Artistic concentration: focuses attention on considerations of the history and the presence of craft in poetry.
- Embodied experience: recognises the need for audiences to *feel* with, rather than about a poem, to experience emotions and feelings in situ.
- Discovery/surprise: the poem teaches us to see something familiar in new ways or ways that might be surprising. We learn something new about the human condition and ourselves.
- Conditional: the partiality of the story should also be recognised through poetry, point of view as conditional whilst presenting what we may call narrative truth.
- Narrative truths: the facts presented should ring true, regardless of whether events, feelings, emotions and images 'actually' happened.
- Transformation: is about providing new insight, giving perspective or advocating for social change.

This poetic tick list could also be applied to other arts-based methods; however, as opposed to 'criteria' (reinforcing the problematising notion of 'criteriology'), we might call them characterised traits (Sparkes and Smith 2009), which are aimed at maintaining a good standard of research that merges artistic and scientific principles. Smith and Caddick's overview of traits for judging qualitative inquiry could be helpful in shaping Poetic Inquiry (Table 7.1).

Table 7.1 Based on Smith and Caddick's (2012, p. 70) list of characterised traits

1. Substantive contribution	Does this piece contribute to our understanding of social life? Does the writer demonstrate a deeply grounded (if embedded) social scientific perspective? How has this perspective informed the construction of the text? (Richardson 2000, p. 937)
2. Impact	Does this affect me? Emotionally? Intellectually? Does it generate new questions? Move me to write? Move me to try new research practices? Move me to action? (Richardson 2000, p. 937)
3. Width	The comprehensiveness of evidence. This dimension refers to the quality of the interview or observations, as well as to the proposed interpretation or analysis. Numerous quotations in reporting narrative studies, as well as suggestions of alternative explanations, should be provided to support the reader's judgment of the evidence and its interpretation (Lieblich et al. 1998, p. 73)
4. Coherence	The way different parts of the interpretation create a complex and meaningful picture. Coherence can be evaluated both internally, in terms of how the parts fit together, and externally, namely against existing theories and previous research (Lieblich et al. 1998, p. 173)
5. Catalytic and tactical authenticity	This refers to the ability of a given inquiry to prompt first, action on the part of the research participants, and second, the involvement of the researcher/evaluator in training participants in specific forms of social and political training if participants desire such training (Lincoln 1995; Guba et al. 2005)
6. Personal narrative and storytelling as an obligation to critique	How do narrative and story enact an ethical obligation to critique subject positions, acts and received notions of expertise and justice within and outside of the work? (Holman Jones 2005, p. 773)

(continued)

Table 7.1 (continued)

7. Resonance	The research influences, affects or moves particular readers or a variety of readers through aesthetic, evocative representations, naturalistic generalisations and transferable findings (Tracy 2010)
8. Credibility	Has the researcher spent a significant amount of time with participants? Were participant reflections on the researcher's interpretations of the data sought? Participant reflections, or what are sometimes known as member checks, can open up a dialogue about the fairness, appropriateness and believability of interpretations offered. As participants reflect, fresh light on the study may also be thrown up, providing a spur for richer and deeper analyses. Participant reflections are, therefore, less a test of research findings or a technique to achieve theory-free knowledge than they are an opportunity for dialogue with participants, reflexive elaboration, critique, feedback, affirmation, disagreement and even collaboration (Tracy 2010)
9. Transparency	Was the research made transparent through, for example, an audit trail? Did another person, acting as a critical friend, scrutinise matters like theoretical preferences, breadth of the interview sample and the process of sorting, choosing, organising and analysing the data? Did a researcher present their interpretations of the data to critical friends who provided a theoretical sounding board to encourage reflection upon, and exploration of, alternative explanations and interpretations as they emerged in relation to the data? (Tracy 2010)

Thinking back to poetry as literature review, a poem could be another way of understanding how we judge arts-based methods and could be a significant way of saving words. It might seem like we have a lot of lists to draw from now, but this only serves to open up possibilities leaving 'space for dialogue, imagination, growth, and improvisation' (Tracy 2010, p. 837) and moves away from criteriological approach (Burke 2016). These traits and lists might not all need to be employed to judge all arts-based methods (and the list is not exhaustive either), but these characterised traits can be used as a flexible guide to judge the Poetic Inquiry and other arts-based methods.

Backlashes

There are frequent 'backlashes' against qualitative inquiry (e.g. see Morse et al. 2009, 1034–1035; Denzin 2009). Specifically, those who engage in these more innovative forms of representing data seem to be targeted. In 2010, Denzin (2010) made a 'call to action' from qualitative researchers to continue to write about 'real' people and position themselves as moral witnesses to the radical changes going on in society. In the field of sport and exercise science, many researchers (e.g. Gilbourne 2010; Smith 1999; Sparkes 1992, 2009) continue to experiment with alternative forms of writing (e.g. creative writing, poetic representations and auto/ethnography). It is this encouragement that inspires me to 'break away from the conventions of social science inscription to experiment with polyvocality, poetry, pastiche, performance and more' (Gergen and Gergen 2002, p. 14) whilst recognising the risks. Gergen and Gergen (2003) reassure us that there is no 'one best way' in the matter of representation, and this book has focused solely on the Poetic Inquiry. Yet, many other creative, artistic modes of expression can produce findings and insights not readily discoverable via more conventional research methods and forms of representation which can change our understanding of how research makes an 'impact' (Gilbourne and Anderson 2011; Owton and Allen-Collinson 2016).

Another risk involved is embedded in the arts, given that poetry has its own way of knowing and making judgments. In Piirto's (2009) chapter, she potently questions: 'Is not the concept of quality and qualification to be taken seriously in arts-based research?' (p. 96). She warns others to respect the domain in which they are located and remember that 'the arts have their own ways' (p. 97). Through her own assessment of her poetry, she draws on poems to discuss how and why some of them might achieve and some of them might be criticised in the world of poetry. She argues that desire is simply not enough; a researcher may wish to convey data poetically, but this does not guarantee an artistic accomplishment. In essence, remember to situate what it is you are doing and avoid making claims that put your work at further risk.

As a result of such criticisms, it is important to recognise that Poetic Inquiry comes with high risks involved. I express the same sentiments as other researchers who have chosen to venture into experimental ways of representing data: 'the risks involved are worth taking because when this genre does work, it provides a powerful means of understanding phenomena in new and exciting ways' (Sparkes et al. 2003, p. 169). I continue to encourage other researchers to venture into arts-based methods and to consider harnessing the power of poetry, using it as a resource for not only understanding their own experiences and the experiences of others but also as a means of communicating this understanding to different audiences. Also, I invite active readers and listeners to consider Poetic Inquiry as an attempt to offer an alternative 'lens through which to view the same scenery' (Sparkes et al. 2003, p. 155).

References

Back, L. (2007). *The Art of Listening.* Oxford: Berg.

Bochner, A. P. (2000). Criteria against ourselves. *Qualitative Inquiry, 6*(2), 266–272.

Burke, S. (2016). Rethinking 'validity' and trustworthiness in qualitative inquiry: How might we judge the quality of qualitative research in sport and exercise sciences? In B. Smith & A. Sparkes (Eds.), *Routledge handbook of qualitative research in sport and exercise* (pp. 330–339). London: Routledge.

Cahnmann-Taylor, M. (2009). The craft, practice, and possibility of poetry in educational research. In M.Prendergast, C. Leggo, and P. Sameshima (Eds.). *Poetic inquiry:Vibrant voices in the social sciences.* Boston: Sense publishers, 13–29.

Clough, P. (2000). Comments on setting criteria for experimental writing. *Qualitative Inquiry, 6*, 278–291.

Dale, G. A. (1996). Existential phenomenology: Emphasizing the experience of the athlete in sport psychology research. *The Sport Psychologist, 10*(4), 307–321.

Denzin, N. (2009). *Qualitative inquiry under fire: Toward a new paradigm dialogue.* Walnut Creek, CA: Left Coast Press.

Denzin, N. (2010). *The qualitative manifesto: A call to arms.* California: Left Coast Press.

Faulkner, S. (2005). *How do you know a good poem? Poetic representation and the case for criteria.* Symposium conducted at the First International Conference of Qualitative Inquiry. Champaign, IL: Urban-Champaign.

Gergen, M., & Gergen, K. (2003). *Social construction: A reader.* London: Sage.

Gergen, M., & Gergen, K. J. (2002). Ethnographic representation as relationship. In A. Bochner & C. Ellis (Eds.), *Ethnographically speaking* (pp. 11–33). Walnut Creek, CA: AltaMira Press.

Gilbourne, D. (2010). The "edge of darkness" and "just in time": Two cautionary tales, two styles, one story. *Qualitative Inquiry, 16*(5), 325–331.

Gilbourne, D., & Anderson, M. (2011). *Critical essays in applied sport psychology*. Champaign: Human Kinetics.

Guba, E.G., & Lincoln, Y.S. (2005). Paradigmatic controversies, contradictions, and emerging confluences. In N. K. Denzin & Y. S. Lincoln (Eds.). *The Sage handbook of qualitative research* (3rd ed., pp. 191–216). Thousand Oaks, CA: Sage.

Hartnett, S. J. (2003). *Incarceration nation: Investigative prison poems of hope and terror*. California, USA: Rowman Altamira.

Holman Jones, S. (2005). Autoethnography: Making the personal political. In. N. K. Denzin & Y. S. Lincoln (Eds.), *Handbook of Qualitative Research* (pp. 763–791).

Hugo, R. (1992). *The Triggering town: Lectures and essays on poetry and writing*. London: Norton & Company Ltd.

Jary, D., & Jary, J. (Eds.). (2005). *Collins dictionary of Sociology*. Harper: Glasgow.

Leavy, P. (2015). *Method meets art: Arts-based research practice*. New York: Guilford Publications.

Lieblich, A., Tuval-Mashiach, R., & Zilber, T. (1998). *Narrative research: Reading, analysis, and interpretation* (vol. 47). Thousand Oaks: Sage.

Lincoln, Y. S. (1995). Emerging criteria for quality in qualitative and interpretive research. *Qualitative Inquiry, 1*(3), 275–289.

Lincoln, Y. S., Lynham, S. A., & Guba, E. G. (2011). Paradigmatic controversies, contradictions, and emerging confluences, revisited. *The Sage Handbook of Qualitative Research, 4*, 97–128.

Morse, J., Coulehan, J., Thorne, S., Bottorff, J., Cheek, J., & Kuzel, A. (2009). Data expressions of expressing data. *Qualitative Health Research, 19*(8), 1034–1035.

Owton, H., & Allen-Collinson, J. (2016). 'It stays with you': Multiple representations of dance and future possibilities. *Qualitative Research in Sport, Exercise and Health, 9*(1), 49–55.

Pelias, R. (2004). *A methodology of the heart: Evoking academic and daily life*. Walnut Creek, CA: AltaMira Press.

Prendergast, M. (2009). Introduction: The phenomena of poetry in research: "Poem is what?" Poetic Inquiry in qualitative social science research. *Poetic Inquiry: Vibrant voices in the social sciences*, pp. 13–29.

Richardson, L. (2000). Writing: A method of inquiry. In N. Denzin & Y. Lincoln (Eds.), *Handbook of Qualitative Research* (2nd ed., pp. 923–948). London: Sage.

Smith, P. (1999). Food truck's party hat. *Qualitative Inquiry, 5*(2), 244–261.

Smith, B., & Caddick, N. (2012). Qualitative methods in sport: A concise overview for guiding social scientific sport research. *Asia Pacific Journal of Sport and Social Science, 1*(1), 60–73.

Smith, J., & Deemer, D. (2000). The problem of criteria in the age of relativism. In N. Denzin & Y. Lincoln (Eds.), *Handbook of qualitative research* (2nd ed., pp. 877–896). London: Sage.

Sparkes, A. (1992). *Research in physical education and sport: Exploring alternative visions.* London: The Falmer Press.

Sparkes, A. (2001). Myth 94: Qualitative researchers will agree about validity. *Qualitative Health Research, 11*(4), 538–552.

Sparkes, A. (2009). Ethnography and the senses: Challenges and possibilities. *Qualitative research in sport and exercise, 1,* 21–35.

Sparkes, A., Nilges, L., Swan, P., & Dowling, F. (2003). Poetic representations in sport and physical education: Insider perspectives. *Sport, Education and Society, 8*(2), 153–177.

Sparkes, A., & Douglas, K. (2007). Making the case for poetic representations: an example in action. *The Sport Psychologist, 21,* 170–190.

Sparkes, A. C., & Smith, B. (2009). Judging the quality of qualitative inquiry: Criteriology and relativism in Action. *Psychology of Sport and Exercise, 10*(5), 491–497.

Stoller, P. (2010). *Sensuous scholarship.* Philadelphia: University of Pennsylvania Press.

Tracy, S. J. (2010). Qualitative quality: Eight "big-tent" criteria for excellent qualitative research. *Qualitative Inquiry, 16*(10), 837–851.

Wolcott, H. (1994). *Transforming qualitative data: Description, analysis, and interpretation.* London: Sage.

CHAPTER 8

Future Possibilities of Poetic Inquiry

Abstract This chapter focuses on the future possibilities for blending Poetic Inquiry with other forms of arts-based methods, in particular, visual methods (e.g. drawing, photography, film). A move to performance explores how these could be employed to reach wider audiences. Another consideration is given to the future of arts-based methods in a neoliberal culture. In consideration of the emerging 'slow scholarship' approach, for arts-based methods, the goal is to move towards collective action 'precisely to resist intensified pressures to do it all and/or intensify elitist structures that make "slowness" possible for some while leaving others slogging in the trenches' (Mountz et al. 2015, p. 14). Strategies are considered to move collectively as a way to resist the fast-paced academic culture that can mean losing future arts-based researchers.

Keywords Visual images · Photography · Drawing · Film · Collage · Slow scholarship

As Denzin (2010) argues, a move to performance has been coupled with a move towards a readiness to experiment with new representational arts-based forms. I have encompassed drawing and poems in an attempt to blend arts-based methods as a way to capture the *whats* and *hows,* aiming to *show* rather than *tell* (Riessman 2008). Multiple arts-based methods explore how different forms might interact with each other and unite to offer new ways of 'knowing' and 'seeing' (Leavy 2009; Phoenix

H. Owton, *Doing Poetic Inquiry*, Palgrave Studies in Creativity and Culture, DOI 10.1007/978-3-319-64577-3_8

2010; Owton 2013). In the next section, I focus on how poetry can be blended with visual images: drawing, photography and video.

Blending Poetry with Visual Images

Poetry and Drawing

Like poetry, visual images are unique and can evoke particular kinds of emotional and visceral responses (Leavy 2015; Phoenix 2010). The acceptance of the visual arts into interdisciplinary methodological innovations is a relatively new phenomenon (Leavy 2015). Increasingly, researchers are using visual images (e.g. Gravestock 2012; Phoenix 2010; Phoenix and Smith 2011) as a part of data analysis as well as a medium to represent data, often with the intent of confronting and challenging stereotypes and prevailing ideologies that normalise them (Leavy 2015). Phoenix and Smith (2011) suggest that the strengths of visual research are in creativity, expressivity and uncertainty.

Like many arts-based methods, representing visual research seems to be a contested area within the field of visual studies (Phoenix 2010). Like Harrison (2002), we might consider whether visual data should be left to speak for itself. Indeed, there are ongoing debates about issues of representation and ranking between *verbal, visual and written* word. There appears to be a ranking of the *written* word over *verbal,* and *verbal* over the *visual* (Richardson 1997; Phoenix 2010). Offering a poem with an artistic representation is not meant to prioritise or value one over the other, but it is aimed at seeing how these forms might interrelate and respond with each other to offer new ways of 'knowing' and 'seeing' (Leavy 2015; Phoenix 2010; Owton 2013). As Szto (2005) points out:

> Whether you are writing with words or with light, you are writing. You are presenting an illustration of the world. Photography documents more accurately than statistics, it is a direct representation of reality." (cited in Szto et al., p. 140)

When thinking about blending arts-based methods, we might consider Chamberlain et al. (2011) argument that multiple methods function smoothly if they are closely aligned.

In my research with sportspeople with asthma, photos elicited were emergent from the researcher-participant interaction where insights were developed and shared. I chose to draw an artistic impression from these photos to *show* some people's stories, particularly because art can tell stories or express an 'aesthetic truth' or feeling (Gold 2007). As such, I chose to draw from these photos to represent participants with narrative art. Below, I share a drawing from one participant's photos (Fig. 8.1).

We might ask whether this drawing can speak for itself, but if we add a title, then perhaps this adds something different to the drawing (Fig. 8.1).

Title: 'It's the buzz'

Owton (2012), Charcoal, 297 x 420 mm, 130gsm white cartridge paper

If I add a poem to the drawing, we might see how this offers new ways of seeing and knowing about asthma and sporting embodiment (Fig. 8.1).

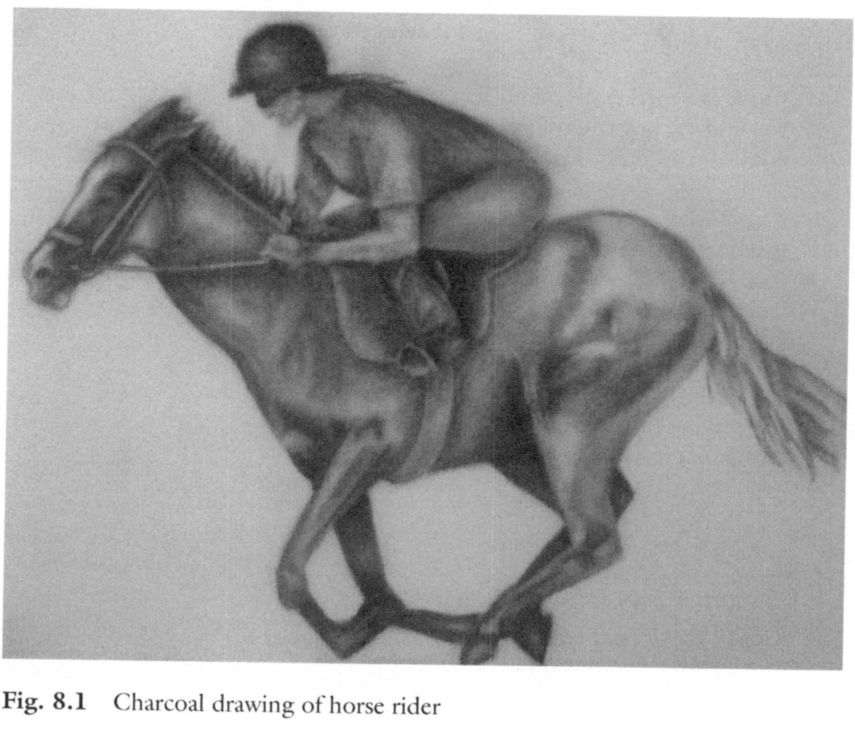

Fig. 8.1 Charcoal drawing of horse rider

It's a buzz

Always wanted to horse ride,
In the forest is where I grew
up, just always wanted to horse ride,

9th birthday present,
Horse riding lessons,
It's what I wanted to do.

Dressage, all about prancing,
Elegant and classical riding,
Horse goes really nicely,
To *school* a horse, getting them almost like dancing,
Not very easy,
So when you *do* actually,
do that and you click and the horse *finally*
does what you want it to do; a *really* good feeling,
Cos the horse has worked well,
you worked well.

You're the teacher,
You and the horse bonding,
Bonded; you're working together.

Race horses; *bit* different,
Just wanna go fast; straight line,
Jockey style riding, you just wanna stay on,
Going fast, going flat out; you get the adrenaline,
Galloping, get the adrenaline rush,
Or on a hunt,
Adrenaline *BUZZ*, teaches you how to ride, to stay on,
Fast; trying to avoid the branches and the holes,
Avoiding everybody,
the *BUZZ* definitely.

I don't worry about anything,
It's just fun,
It's hard work, strenuous; the horses pull,
Got to watch where you're going,
Got to always be thinking,

Not supposed to get in front of the hounds; in front of the certain huntsmen,
Thinking about what you're doing,
Not just like galloping around...
no...
it's good,
It's just fun.

Sneezing doesn't start while I'm *on* the horses back,
In the car coming back,
I sneeze and sneeze and sneeze,
Stream and sneeze, sneeze and stream and sneeze,
Achoo, achoo, achoo,
I sneeze so much, my stomach hurts the next day,
Dust and hay; sets my asthmaAsthma off more than anything else.

The more I go, the less allergic I am,
If I haven't been a while, around horses, then I'm *really* allergic,
My asthma's alright riding; mostly I can.

Done a bit of running; don't do that anymore,
Sore knees, struggled getting fit,
Done a bit of body combat; don't do that anymore,
No other physical activity
really...

Horse riding; means a lot,
I haven't been for a while..,
I really *miss* it,
I wouldn't wanna give it up,
I'd miss it. I enjoy it,
To do; gotta have something,
Otherwise you just sit,
Outside work; gotta have something,
It means a lot.

Then, we might go back to the original question about whether art can speak for itself.

Nonetheless, by asking my participants to provide a photo that was meaningful to them, it offered an opportunity for them to use their bodies and the space around them to *show* rather than just *tell* about their lives (see Riessman 2008). Whilst Westcott (2007) highlights that drawings as opposed to photographs can allow participants to shape how they see themselves and are potentially seen by others, drawings done by the researcher can provide visual interpretation and representation, offering a co-constructed creation developed from the researcher's drawing from the photo elicitation. Gold (2007) uses predominantly photography; he places a high value on researcher-created visual data as a way of 'gaining orientation' and forcing fieldworkers to engage and empathise with participants. Chamberlain et al. (2011) argue that multiple methods encourages creativity and innovation, extends the scope and depth of data, demands time, forces reflexivity, deepens and intensifies relationships between researchers and participants and raises issues of analysis and interpretation, which I previously highlighted. Given the fluid nature of identity, poems and art also reject static or unitary meaning and instead reveal the multiplicity of meanings (Leavy 2015).

> The increasing popularity of qualitative methodologies in the study of health, illness and health care has reflected an epistemological commitment to the ways participants themselves interpret, give meaning to and make sense of, their experiences. These might be 'ordinary' everyday experiences and events, or those which disrupt and require new responses from both self and others, including the construction of new identities (Harrison 2002, p. 864).

By encompassing a multitude of different forms/representations, they might provide specific information about our existence and act as powerful indicators regarding multiple meanings embedded within our culture (Phoenix 2010). Therefore, by mixing alternative and multiple methods, arts-based methods are aimed at exploring personal and shared bodily felt sensory experiences as well as other overlooked issues such as the *meanings* people give their lives.

Poetry and Photography

We can explore similar debates about representations in poetry and photography. Photography, however, has been employed as an explicit research tool in social research for a longer period of time than poetry (Szto et al. 2005). Szto et al. (2005) explore how photography and poetry might provide insight and understanding into human behaviour and the social world. It continues to act as an important documentation of the social world and can add another layer to research (Ellis 2001). Photography can link the image to the viewers resonating their emotive connection to the human condition (Szto et al. 2005). Like the poet-researcher, the photographer is an ethnographer capturing the reality of the social world; therefore, photography is research (Szto et al. 2005). Consider how a poem and photo might align to provide new insights and even enhance the accuracy of the account. I explore three poems that I have written and include photos to explore what new insights and understandings might transpire (Fig. 8.2).

(Owton 2012)

Fig. 8.2 Photo of dad

20 Years Later...

Spreading the world with what you left me,
In a squeezed time-frame,
All the proverbs on your office cupboard door,
Kept treasured; enveloped in my memory,
Opening when opportunities face me.

Eyes smiling; you live through us,
Paying lip service; my spiritual reliance,
Working all the hours; sacrificial consequence,
Family business importance,
Windsurfing was your escape; always trying to balance,

"Sitting on the dock of the bay"
Taking opportune moments.

Not a man of many words,
That's what people say,
and what I remember,
Only if things were absurd!
Recession attacked your heart!
For educational significance.

"Oooo, that's why I'm easy,
I'm easy like Sunday morning"

It's not always easy...
because you're *not* here and you still *died* Daddy.

Faultless; in my heart
Gazing at the stars,
still feeling your presence anyway.

See Fig 8.3.

This Brave Tree

In this garden, there was this brave tree; years it stood,
Grounded in the earth,
Built strength from just a foot,
Started to grow, no lack of collective dearth.
Branches out in different directions,

Fig. 8.3 Photo of de-rooted tree

yet maintained workable roots.
Built an esteemed reputation,
Safely? Embedded in its place, surrounded by different groups,
Internationally known.

Suddenly, subjected to tempestuous changes,
Garden unforgivably fails to protect it.
Left exposed to weather the storm, garden rearranges,
Destruction of the tree inevitable; every precious bit.

Welted leaves blown away,
Sturdy branches slowly break,
The storm is brutal in every way,
Rain drip drops off the twigs into the lake.
All that's left is a rotting stump,
When the tempest's over, there'll be a wake,
Everyone'll say to the garden dump,
"You let it die, for fuck's sake!"

Fig. 8.4 Photo of blossoming tree

See Fig. 8.4.

This Brave Tree II

This tree; subjected to tempestuous changes,
This tree's garden unforgivably failing to protect it,
Left exposed to weather the storm, garden rearranges,
Destruction of the tree inevitable; every precious bit

I saw this tree fall into an empty pit…

I felt this tree's emotional drain
Through all the never ending pitiful rain
Flooded; I felt this tree's shame
As it lay on the floor feeling legless, naked, exposed, lame

I felt this tree's pain, tattooing markings deep into its body
Weltered as it tried to shave away it's history, wash away it's memory

I felt this tree's self-esteem
disintegrate; getting washed away in a silent stream

I watched this sobering tree slowly crawl back to reality
I watched this brave tree start to work on its recovery
I watched this honest tree slowly begin to accept
a slow un-denial of a true authenticity as it started reconstructing it's identity

I watch as this tree sews new seeds,
branches re-grow, re-rooting nurturing to be
this tree to find another
to love others just as much as I love this tree

you know… I have a feeling that this tree
I'm starting to love
That got saved
… is really me

Blending Poetry with Video

Another way to breathe life into experience is to employ video representation as a research tool. During work on a paper about the grooming process and sexual abuse in sport (Owton and Sparkes 2017), I wanted to breathe life into what the process was like for my participant (Bella) as well as show the experience of engaging with the process of collaborative research in sensitive topics. In the video (link: https://www.youtube.com/watch?v=f_R6EQXEKV8), I include a poem written by Bella and blend this with images and music. By weaving, orchestrating and spacing visuals and music to explore a research topic, this type of approach is aimed at stimulating dialogue and is a powerful method to survey a current topic combining creative work and critical studies with individual expression and aesthetic reflection.

Video representation, as an arts-based method, assumes an attitude of persuasiveness and is intended to be a communicative tool for social justice to help us see things in new and unanticipated ways giving a voice to taboo topics that are often silenced. Increasingly, researchers are conducting research via the arts to break out of the conventional; hence,

I argue that to become a researcher who fuses the arts into research processes and representations is to possess a creativity and artfulness. Indeed, to engage in the process of this work is 'to act as a visual artist, poet, photographer, performer, filmmaker and so on' (Knowles and Promislow 2008, p. 519), which makes my 'self' visible in the research process. Like McNiff (2008, p. 30), when I have shared my drawings, poems and videos with my participants 'researching human experience through the arts makes complete sense to people' and can feel 'more accurate, original, and intelligent than more conventional descriptions'.

Kip Jones has drawn on video to show various topics that he has researched. He blends poetry with video in 'I remember the Night' (2009: https://vimeo.com/4352507) which tells the story of a 65-year-old woman in the UK recalling the turning point as a child when her parents asked her which one she wanted to live with. He uses three different voices to capture how the traumatic event became a lasting memory through various stages in her ('Polly') life. Since then, he has produced a 30-minute film (with Director Josh Appignanesi) called 'Rufus Stone' (link: https://vimeo.com/109360805) exploring ageing and gay life in rural South West England and Wales. Of course, the cost of such a film needs to be accommodated for and could restrict others from producing such a film; however, 'I remember the night' was not costly. Videos are accessible to wider audiences and provide a version of a truth to be let out into the public for discussion and dialogue, in this case, about gay and ageing lives.

Other ways to employ video is via an ethno-documentary style. Andrew Stephenson (2015) employed video to explore four friendships in relation to places, spaces, urban landscapes and mind-body-world interconnections; it's called 'How we know each other' (link: https://vimeo.com/130013072). Anderson (2012) produced a 20-minute documentary about a gay-basketball team called 'Purple Shoelaces' (link: https://vimeo.com/44900875). Kitrina Douglas and David Carless have employed video representations including song writing, music, poetry and a combination of effects to represent research on various topics. Their first video called Gwithian Sands (2013a, link: https://www.youtube.com/watch?v=IuUFDMLGfiE) is a short music documentary from their research exploring the lives, physical activity and experiences of women over 60 years of age living in Cornwall. They have a number of videos accessible to the public, and I list a few more examples here:

- The Long Run (2014) about mental health and physical activity. It is a runner's story of living with severe and ongoing mental health problems (link: https://www.youtube.com/watch?v=v-fprKKUGKo)
- These Things (2015) about an elderly preferred housing scheme (link: https://www.youtube.com/watch?v=ZHFfa1Opm9w)
- The Blue Funnel Line (2015) tracing the journey of a merchant seaman from Liverpool who worked on the Blue Funnel Line which was born out of life history research with supported housing in Bristol (link: https://www.youtube.com/watch?v=cftAy_SaurY)

With discussions around impact in academia, it is important to recognise the wide audience that arts-based methods have the potential to reach. The examples above show that there are different ways to create a video and there is no right way. There are lots of ways to be creative and capture the research in a powerful, evocative, insightful and different way. Whilst arts-based methods might be a barrier because they do not feel 'qualified' enough, videos can create another barrier about not feeling/being technical enough. Not all researchers are artists or feel confident in their 'creative' and/or 'technical' abilities so you might think about collaborating with others who could bring your research to life in different ways. When producing a video think about the following:

- Who is your audience? (e.g. academic, public and professional)
- What theme do you want to capture? (e.g. a theme within a topic)
- How can you make it authentic? (e.g. voices)
- How can you blend arts-based methods together so that they are aligned? (e.g. poetry and music)
- What sounds will you include? (e.g. speaking, voices, music, songs and train sounds)
- What images will you include? (e.g. pictures, photos and moving footage)
- The length of film that will capture your audience
- Where will you release the video? (e.g. academic journal, youtube and vimeo)

Poetry with Collage Inquiry

Another visual method is collage. Collage comes from the French word—coller—meaning to stick. Collage refers to the genre where materials are found, stuck or pasted on some sort of surface. Collage dates back at least 1000 years in folk art and challenges the long-term conventions of painting. Collage as inquiry can be employed as a helpful way of conceptualising a response to a research question and could be blended with poetry to produce new insights. Alternatively, a series of collages can be created to respond to the question or when working as a team, each of the researchers can produce a collage in response to a research question. The results can then be analysed using viewing, discussing and writing in order to find commonalities and difference amongst the collages to conceptualise the nuances of the phenomenon. Blending this with poetry would add a multifaceted layering of insights. When employing collage as inquiry, it might be useful to think about the following:

- The role of colour
- Texture
- Size
- Directionality
- Space
- Position in composition
- Mixing and matching photos/writing/letters

Helen Clegg, Jacquelyn Allen-Collinson and I are employing collage as inquiry (Butler-Kisber 2008) to engage the boys in discussion and as a unique way to understand and represent the boys' meanings in dance. Indeed, as Butler-Kisber (2008) argues, collage can be used as a helpful way of conceptualising a response to a research question (e.g. what does dance mean to you?). We could blend collage as inquiry with participant-transcribed poems to offer new and alternative insights. Also, body sculpting will be used as a way for the boys to express their feelings and thoughts about what dance means to them. Body sculpting was originally used in family therapy as a way of allowing individuals to express their feelings and emotions about a topic within their family context (Papp et al. 2013). This is a particularly effective method for dancers to express themselves given that such techniques are used in dance, especially contemporary dance, and so will not be unfamiliar to many of the participants. Body sculptures within this study will be formed by the participants forming sculptures with their own bodies in relation to the other participants around them exploring what dance means to them. This sculpture will also be part of the data as a visual collage of bodies. Other novel approaches include camera-based 'moving methods' (Palmer 2016) and video diaries (Bates 2013; Cherrington and Watson 2010), Once the door has been opened, there are many creative possibilities available when employing arts-based methods. Taking a phenomenologically inspired approach lends itself well to an open 'go with the flow' approach to enable such creative possibilities to emerge in research.

The Poetic Effect

As humans, we are constantly reinventing our world and ourselves, and it is still possible to say something new, or perhaps something old in a *new* or novel way by using new forms, new ideas in language and infusing the truly new world of science/art/technology/reality with the very, very old questions of humanity (Hogue 2006). However, Hogue (2006) argues that there must be some reason other than just the *process* of writing poems. Alternatively, *themes* express the unity of human experience, and through poems, we see that we are more alike as a human race than different (Hogue 2006): *What makes us all the same is that we are all different.*

> The world consigns its myths, its religions, its dreams and deepest feelings to poetry for safekeeping: and somehow, even its critics and doubters know where to find it in time of need (Boran, 25th March Boran 2012).

There are moments in life when we feel a sense of belonging—there is a sense of togetherness when standing, sitting, jumping in a crowd and watching athletes who excite, enlighten and inspire you. I want you to *feel* the lines of poetry in your veins flowing through your body, in your heart washing you with emotion and in your soul reminding you of your moral humane duty to feel compassion. I want you to *experience* the poems viscerally, *remember* them in the windows of your 'dramaturgical' imagination, *think* about them and *reflect* on them. I also want you to 'get to know' the participants so that you can engage more personally with the data.

Gravestock (2012) argues that drawing, if applied effectively, has the potential to enhance research methods in the field of sport and exercise science. And here I provide multiple feedback from some of my participants to demonstrate the effectiveness of these representations and the emotional bonds between us.

> I am fascinated by your use of artwork and poetry in your analysis. I think you are on to something really special here! Seeing images of contributors allows a greater degree of connection (even if only imaginary) with the contributor responses. I believe that we are actually very good at connecting with aspects of people through their images in ways not open through the words alone. Some iconic images (Einstein's sticking his tongue out for example) give a much more rounded understanding of people best known by their written work.
>
> I think you're doing something that goes beyond being brave and that strikes me as so very admirable—it actually allows a whole new means of tapping into emotional response to information—or at least an ancient bardic means of tapping into the emotional content of information. [...] The phrasing, pauses and stylistic mannerisms transport me much more into my imagination and to experience more vividly the tale being told. The information being imparted is far richer and potent. This heightened experience of an emotionally painful story is what caught me out with your last poem [...] you are really getting to me with your poems and I can see how powerful your approach is. Comfortable, no! But you are really onto something different and I hope that the strong emotional response you get from people doesn't put you off.

Indeed, poetry is relational, and I take every poem back to the participants to check that the poem is an accurate and respectful representative of their experience. I am reassured on every occasion and provide some responses from my participants below:

> I really appreciated your last poem - and it was a little unexpected so it hurt a little to read it. Nevertheless, it captured my feelings very well so well done on your listening skills!
>
> That really is it. That really encapsulates everything. Yes.
>
> You didn't re-traumatise me but it was kind of reading it, felt like a bit of a saga which I had kind of forgotten. It reminded me of how traumatising

it was. The effect it might have on others of your condition. It was a *felt* experience. I liked it.

It was fun to read and also added something to the tale that almost made a humdrum everyday experience just a little like some ancient bard's tale.

It is so accurate.

Many thanks for sending the poem. I think you've caught an atmosphere, brilliantly, and it's very sensitive. I'm pleased to have a copy.

Poetic representations seem to touch participants on an emotional level, which can connect researcher and participant in new and unanticipated ways: a powerful force and energy exchange between researcher and participant. As Szto et al. (2005, p. 138) state:

> Artists and qualitative researchers both strive for authentic relationships with the external world based upon the commitment to portray the experiences of others in an honest, accurate manner. They both explore the unknown, and hope that such knowledge will lead to the betterment of personkind.

Pelias (2011) desires a relational language through poetry and, like him, I want 'to enter a space that can be shared, to invite and to be invited' (p. 227). *Leaning in*to participant's stories and sharing poetry and artistic impressions seem to have enabled this connection and relational being to (co)exist between participant and researcher.

Dare to care

Could you dare to care? Could you feel what's real?
None of that pretending shit,
That superficial self-serving sympathetic shit,
That 'I know how you feel' patronising shit,
That fake politically correct condescending shit...

Really to *feel* what it's like to care?

A lot of people find it easier,
To not listen, not believe, not feel,
Minds deluded; objectively clearer,
What's kind of known as a denier.

Don't turn away from that street guy begging,
Abuse; that kid suffering, strangers crying… arms hugging,
Don't always switch off from 'negative' ranting,
That old woman mumbling,
Don't be ignorant, afraid of prying,
Discomfort when bruises seeing; self-injurying.

Stop giving into these dyer deadly illusionary happy distractions,
Stop striving for meaningless media validation.

Can you ever be waking?
Taking stock; sceptically pausing, un-brainwashed; freshly looking,
With your eyes wide opening, obsessive ears; listening… *Really* questioning.

Don't just sympathise,
Don't just pay lip service,
to empathy – recognise,
Feel it wrenching at your heart, empathise.

Embody experience emotionally,
Physically, mentally, bravely,
Mind-body; re-engaging, listening,
Flesh, skin and bones,
Desperate pleading moans.

Dare to care
If you can bare the pain; life's unfair.

Next time you're asking, *'How are you doing?'*
Try listening, try double-checking,
Ditch your high class technological blanket of safety; risk the un-distracting,
Try, just try caring.

Commensurate with a phenomenologically inspired approach, arts-based methods provide diverse openings to explore sensorial experiential aspects (Owton 2015a, Allen-Collinson and Hockey 2006; Sparkes and Smith 2014) and different modes of performance (Carless 2011;

Carless and Douglas 2014; Douglas 2012; Douglas and Carless 2008; Douglas and Carless 2013b; Owton 2015b; McMahon 2016; Gergen and Gergen 2016; Saldaña 2008; Blumenfeld-Jones 2008; Donmoyer and Donmoyer 2008; Bresler 2008). If we dare, there are vast possibilities for seeing how multi-layered arts-based methods might be intertextually interconnected and form new and insightful meanings (Owton and Allen-Collinson 2016).

Slow Movement

In the UK, the government appears to be intensifying the paradigms debate which makes it even more difficult for arts-based methods to be accepted. The privatisation of the arts, humanities and social sciences in England could mean that the struggle will only get worse for these fields of inquiry as they are downgraded to 'non-priority' status. For such a short-term gain, it could mean that we will likely have a missing generation of artists and researchers who failed to receive the small amounts of funding needed to provide unique insights. With enforced targets and overpowering budget cuts from the government, it seems even more important, but even more difficult, to nurture creative and innovative research.

Language has changed to accommodate the movement towards offering objective, measurable criteria (Hussey and Smith 2010). Hussey and Smith (2010) argue that a 'language of machine' serves to dehumanise the whole experience of education and 'as language changes, so does thinking, and as thinking changes so does action and with it the whole experience of education' (Hussey and Smith 2010, p. 22). Instead, we need to celebrate rather than stifle creativity (Owton and Allen-Collinson 2016) by drawing from new and imaginative judgement criteria to accommodate these types of research (Barone and Eisner 2012). Additionally, future possibilities for arts-based methods could, however, be under threat (Owton and Allen-Collinson 2016). Not only does good scholarship require time: time to think, write, read, research, analyse, edit and collaborate (Mountz et al. 2015), but arts-based methods also require thinking and studio space (Leavy 2015). Indeed, arts-based methods challenge us as researchers to:

> …not so quickly select a comfortable way to create and share research, but rather let the inquiry's focus, the data's form, the audience's perspectives, and our inner muse guide us to consider new alternatives (Chenail 2015).

Whilst Poetic Inquiry is calling for researchers to slow down, live in the moment and breathe—fully urging for a uniting of the heart, mind, imagination, body and spirit, which requires the perception of space in the mind, energy, positivity and connectivity; the British higher education system has been working against this ethos. A neoliberal university culture encourages speed and 'fast' work which has forced academics to try and find remedies (Owton and Allen-Collinson 2016). Creative academic research and practice, however, requires 'slow work' which is not a form of laziness but is about approaching research with care and attention (Parkins and Craig 2006). O'Reilley reminds us to stop abusing ourselves with overwork because it can ruin our health and make us dislike students. Instead, many have started to call for a 'slow movement' (Berg and Seeber 2016; Lawthom 2015; Mountz et al. 2015; Owton and Allen-Collinson 2016) in academia in order to work collaboratively and 'live in the present in a meaningful, sustainable, thoughtful and *pleasurable* way' (Parkins and Craig 2006, p. ix). Strategies for 'slow' scholarship 'favours deep reflexive thought, engaged research, joy in writing and working with concepts and ideas driven by our passions' (Mountz et al. 2015, p. 19). Additionally, the slow scholarship movement seeks to enable:

> a feminist ethics of care that allows us to claim some time as our own, build shared tie into everyday life, and help buffer each other from unrealistic and counterproductive norms that have become standard expectations (Mountz et al. 2015, p. 19).

'Slow work' is required to produce good scholarship but it 'both defies and is threatened by the myriad demands of our time as academic laborers' (Mountz et al. 2015, p. 3). For those wanting to engage in Poetic Inquiry or other arts-based methods, it demands that we work against the time-starved neoliberal culture (Owton and Allen-Collinson 2016; Allen-Collinson 2009). In relation to a phenomenologically inspired approach, as argued:

> As qualitative researchers in these subject areas, we are often particularly highly attuned to the embodied consequences for our participants of being placed in highly demanding and stressful situations. Many of us undertake research that aims to improve the health and wellbeing of others, including athletes, sportswo/men (at all levels) and exercisers, and to challenge

> and critique social-structural constraints that have such negative impacts upon individuals and social groups. Being confronted daily and routinely by ever-mounting performativity pressures in the academic life-world can certainly generate deleterious corporeal effects and affects for us and for our colleagues across all disciplinary areas. We contend that for arts-based methods to have a valued future in our subject area, we may need to move towards collective action (Owton and Allen-Collinson 2016, p. 53).

This collective action requires institutions to create supportive working environments that value recognition and appreciate non-work aspects of life actively working to buffer workers against the risks of burnout (Westring 2014; Wu 2015) and other health-compromising risks (Owton and Allen-Collinson 2016). As Meyerhoff et al. (2011) argue, this requires more than just making 'more time' for arts-based methods, but working to 'change' time to enable academics to 'challenge and critique the practices by which universities harness the creative time of labour, and develop a revolutionary theory of time that enables us to see capital not as the generative source of innovation, but rather as parasitic upon it' (Owton and Allen-Collinson 2016, p. 53).

References

Allen-Collinson, J. (2009). Negative 'marking': University research administrators and the contestation of moral exclusion. *Studies in Higher Education, 34*(8), 941–954.

Anderson. (2012). *Purple shoelaces*. Available: https://vimeo.com/44900875.

Barone, T., & Eisner, E. W. (2012). *Art-based research*. London: Sage.

Bates, C. (2013). Video diaries: Audio-visual research methods and the elusive body. *Visual Studies, 28*(1), 29–37.

Berg, M., & Seeber, B. (2016). *Slow professor: Challenging the culture of speed in the Academy*. Toronto: University of Toronto Press.

Blumenfeld-Jones, D. (2008). Dance, choreography, and social science research. In A. Cole & G. Knowles (Eds.). *Handbook of the Arts in Qualitative Research*, 175–184.

Boran, P. (2012). *Sue Boynton Poetry Contest*. [Online, 25 March, 2012]. Available: http://boyntonpoetrycontest.wordpress.com/tag/pat-boran/. Accessed 24 Sept 2012.

Bresler, L. (2008). The music lesson. In A. Cole & G. Knowles (Eds.). *Handbook of the Arts in Qualitative Research*, 225–237.

Butler-Kisber, L. (2008). Collage as inquiry. In J. G. Knowles & A. L. Cole (Eds.). *Handbook of the arts inqualitative research* (pp. 265–276). Thousand Oaks, CA: Sage.

Carless, D., & Douglas, K. (2014). *The long run*. Available from: https://www.youtube.com/watch?v=v-fprKKUGKo.

Carless, D. (2011). What's in a song? How songs contribute to the communication of social science research. *British Journal of Guidance and Counselling, 39*(5), 439–454.

Chamberlain, K., Cain, T., Sheridan, J., & Dupuis, A. (2011). Pluralisms in qualitative research: From multiple methods to integrated methods. *Qualitative Research in Psychology, 8*, 151–169.

Chenail, R. (2015). In P. Leavy (Ed.). *Method meets art: Arts-based research practice*. New York: Guilford Publications.

Cherrington, J., & Watson, B. (2010). Shooting a diary, not just hoop: Using video diaries to explore the embodied, everyday contexts of a university basketball team. *Qualitative Research in Sport and Exercise, 2*(2), 267–281.

Denzin, N. (2010). *The Qualitative manifesto: A call to arms*. Walnut Creek, CA: Left Coast Press.

Donmoyer, R., & Donmoyer, J. Y. (2008). Readers' theater as a data display strategy. In A. Cole & G. Knowles (Eds.). *Handbook of the arts in qualitative research: Perspectives, methodologies, examples, and issues*, pp. 209–224.

Douglas, K., & Carless, D. (2008). Nurturing a performative self. *Forum: Qualitative social research, 9*(2), Art 23.

Douglas, K. (2012). Signals and signs. *Qualitative Inquiry, 18*(6), 525–532.

Douglas, K., & Carless, D. (2013a). *Gwithian sands*. Available: https://www.youtube.com/watch?v=IuUFDMLGfiE.

Douglas, K., & Carless, D. (2013b). An invitation to performative research. *Methodological Innovations Online, 8*(1), 1–12.

Douglas, K and Carless, D. (2015). *The Blue funnel*. Available:https://www.youtube.com/watch?v=cftAy_SaurY.

Douglas, K and Carless, D. (2015). *These Things*. Available:https://www.youtube.com/watch?v=ZHFfa1Opm9w.

Ellis, C. (2001). With mother/with child: A true story. *Qualitative Inquiry, 7*(5), 598–616.

Gergen, M. M., & Gergen, K. J. (2016). *Playing with purpose: Adventures in performative social science*. New York: Routledge.

Gold, S. (2007). Using photography in studies of immigrant communities. In G. Stanczak (Ed.). *Visual research methods: Image, society and representation*. London: Sage.

Gravestock, H. (2012). Embodying understanding: Drawing as research in sport and exercise. In *Presentation at British Psychological Society conference*.

Harrison, B. (2002). Seeing health and illness worlds—Using visual methodologies in a sociology of health and illness: A methodological review. *Sociology of Health & Illness, 24*(6), 856–872.

Hogue, D. (2006). *What is a poem made of?* Available: http://www.mshogue.com/poetry/made_of.html. Accessed 11 Apr 2011.

Hussey, T., and Smith, P. (2010). *The trouble with higher education: a critical examination of our universities.*London: Routledge.

Jones, K. (2009). *I remember that night.* Available: https://www.vimeo.com/4352507.

Knowles, J. G., & Promislow, S. (2008). Using an arts methodology to create a thesis or dissertation. In A. Cole & G. Knowles (Eds.). *Handbook of the arts in qualitative research: Perspectives, methodologies, examples and issues* (pp. 511–527). Thousand Oaks, CA: Sage.

Lawthom, R. (2015). Keynote: Women in, through, within science: Walls, ceilings, communities and colonies. In *Psychology of women's section conference*, 10 July 2015, Windsor Cumberland Lodge.

Leavy, P. (2009). Fractured femininities/massacred masculinities: A poetic installation. *Qualitative Inquiry, 15*(9), 1439–1447.

Leavy, P. (2015). *Method meets art: Arts-based research practice.* New York: Guilford.

McMahon, J. (2016). Creative analytical practices. Qualitative interviewing in the sport and exercise sciences. In Smith, B. M & Sparkes, A. C. (Eds.). *Routledge handbook of qualitative research in sport and exercise* (pp. 302–315).

McNiff, S. (2008). Art-based research. *Handbook of the Arts in Qualitative Research*, 29–40.

Meyerhoff, E., Johnson, E., & Braun, B. (2011). Time and the university. *ACME: An International E-journal for Critical Geographies, 10*(3), 483–507.

Mountz, A., et al. (2015). For slow scholarship: A feminist politics of resistance through collective action in the neoliberal university. *ACME: An International E-journal for Critical Geographies, 14*(4), 1235–1259.

Owton, H. (2012). Streams of bereavement. *Qualitative Inquiry, 20*, 1–4.

Owton, H. (2013). Integrating multiple forms of representation: Fighting asthma. *Qualitative Inquiry, 19*, 601–604.

Owton, H. (2015a). Performative embodiment and unravelling grandparent–grandchild relationships. *Qualitative Inquiry, 21*(5), 426–435.

Owton, H. (2015b). *Learning from Bella's story.* Available: https://www.youtube.com/watch?v=f_R6EQXEKV8.

Owton, H., & Allen-Collinson, J. (2016). 'It stays with you': Multiple representations of dance and future possibilities. *Qualitative Research in Sport, Exercise and Health, 9*(1), 49–55.

Owton, H., & Sparkes, A. (2017). Sexual abuse and the grooming process in sport: Bella's story. *Sport, Education and Society* [Online early]. Available http://www.tandfonline.com/doi/abs/10.1080/13573322.2015.1063484.

Palmer, C. (2016). Research on the run: Moving methods and the charity 'thon'. *Qualitative research in sport, exercise and health, 8*(3), 225–236.

Papp, P., Scheinkman, M., & Malpas, J. (2013). Breaking the mold: Sculpting impasses in couples' therapy. *Family Process, 52*(1), 33–45.

Parkins, W., & Craig, G. (2006). *Slow living*. Oxford: Berg.

Pelias, R. J. (2016). *Leaning: A poetics of personal relations*. London: Routledge.

Phoenix, C. (2010). Seeing the world of physical culture: The potential of visual methods for qualitative research in sport and exercise. *Qualitative Research in Sport and Exercise, 2*(2), 93–108.

Phoenix, C., & Smith, B. (2011). *The world of physical culture in sport and exercise: Visual methods for qualitative research*. London: Routledge.

Richardson, L. (1997). *Fields of play: Constructing an academic life*. New Brunswick, NJ: Rutgers University Press.

Riessman, C. K. (2008). *Narrative methods for the human sciences*. Thousand Oaks, CA: Sage.

Saldaña, J. (2008). The drama and poetry of qualitative method. In A. Cole & G. Knowles (Eds.). *Handbook of the arts in qualitative research*, 195–208.

Stephenson, A. (2015). How we know each other: A film about four friendships, screened as part of ESRC festival of social science, November 2015. Brooks Building, Manchester Metropolitan University.

Szto, P., Furman, R., & Langer, C. (2005). Poetry and photography: An exploration into expressive/creative qualitative research. *Qualitative Social Work, 4*(2), 135–156.

Westcott, E. (2007). *Shadow of darkness*. Unpublished thesis, University of Exeter, UK.

Westring, A. (2014). New research: A supportive culture buffers women from the negative effects of long hours. *Harvard Business Review*. Available from: https://hbr.org/2014/02/new-research-a-supportive-culture-buffers-women-from-thenegative-effects-of-long-hours.

Wu, C. (2015). Tenured and happy. *Inside higher education*. Available from: https://www.insidehighered.com/advice/2015/03/30/essay-earning-tenure-and-considering-responsibilities-faculty-life.

Bibliography

Allen-coll, E., & Hoehn, K. (2007). *Human Anatomy and Physiology*. (7th ed.). London: Pearson.

Archer, L. (2012). Between authenticity and pretension: Parents', pupils' and young professionals' negotiations of minority ethnic middle-class identity. *The Sociological Review, 60*(1), 129–148.

Canivet, C., Östergren, P. O., Lindeberg, S. I., Choi, B., Karasek, R., Moghaddassi, M., et al. (2010). Conflict between the work and family domains and exhaustion among vocationally active men and women. *Social Science & Medicine, 70*(8), 1237–1245.

Carless, D. (2012). Negotiating sexuality and masculinity in school sport: An autoethnography. *Sport, Education and Society, 17*(5), 607–625.

Collins. Johnson, N. (2009). The role of self and emotion within qualitative sensitive research: A reflective account. *Enquire*, 4, 23–50.

Douglas, K., & Carless, D. (2014). The long run. Available: https://www.youtube.com/watch?v=v-fprKKUGKo.

Douglas, K., & Carless, D. (2015). The blue funnel. Available: https://www.youtube.com/watch?v=cftAy_SaurY.

Douglas, K., & Carless, D. (2015). These things. Available: https://www.youtube.com/watch?v=ZHFfa1Opm9w.

Furman, R. (2004). Poetic forms and structures in qualitative health research. *Qualitative Health Research, 16*(4), 560–566.

Furman, R., Langer, C., Davis, C., Gallardo, H. P., & Kulkarni, S. (2007). Expressive research and reflective poetry as qualitative inquiry: A study of adolescent identity. *Qualitative Research, 7*(3), 301–315.

Hanauer, D. (2010). Poetry as research. John Benjamins Publishing Company.

H. Owton, *Doing Poetic Inquiry*, Palgrave Studies in Creativity and Culture, DOI 10.1007/978-3-319-64577-3

Hanisch, C. (2006). *The personal is political: The women's liberation movement classic with a new explanatory introduction.* Available: http://www.carolhanisch.org/CHwritings/PIP.html Accessed 19 Apr 2017.

Hanks, T. (2016). Tom hanks says self-doubt is 'A high-wire act that we all walk'. *NPR.org.* Available: http://www.npr.org/2016/04/26/475573489/tom-hanks-says-self-doubt-is-a-high-wire-act-that-we-all-walk Accessed 18 Apr 2017.

Hochschild, A. (1979). Emotion work, feeling rules, and social structure. *American Journal of Sociology, 85,* 551–575.

Hussey, T., & Smith, P. (2010). *The trouble with higher education: A critical examination of our universities.* London: Routledge.

Jones, K. (1998). I remember that night. Available: https://vimeo.com/4352507.

Jones, K. (2014). Rufus stone. Available: https://vimeo.com/109360805 Accessed 26 Apr 2017.

Josselson, R. (1995). *The space between us: Exploring the dimensions of human relationships.* Sage.

Klemola, T. (1991). Dance and embodiment. *Ballet International, 1,* 1–16. Available: http://files.kotisivukone.com/finevision.kotisivukone.com/tiedostot/dance_and_embodyment.pdf. Accessed 31 Apr 14.

MacCaig, N. (1989). *An ordinary day.* In *The new dragon book of verse.* Oxford: Oxford University Press.

Marieb, E.N., & Hoehn K. (2007). *Human Anatomy and Physiology.* (7th ed.). London: Pearson.

Martell, L. (2014, September). The slow university: Inequality, power and alternatives. In *Forum qualitative sozialforschung/forum: Qualitative social research 15*(3).

Owton, H. (2011). Granny's memoirs: He thought it was paradise. *Qualitative Inquiry,* XX, pp. 1–2.

Proust, M. (2006). *Remembrance of things past* (trans. C. K. Scott Moncrieff). Hertfordshire: Wordsworth Editions.

Schmitt, R. (2005). Systematic metaphor analysis as a method of qualitative research. *The Qualitative Report, 10*(2), 358–394.

Tedlock, D. (2011). *The spoken word and the work of interpretation.* University of Pennsylvania Press.

Wilde, O. (1972). *The story of an unhappy friendship: With portraits and facsimile letters.* London: The Hermes Press.

Young, I. M. (1998). Throwing like a girl: Twenty years later. In D. Welton (Ed.), *Body and flesh: A philosophical reader* (pp. 286–290). Oxford: Blackwell.

Index

H. Owton, *Doing Poetic Inquiry*, Palgrave Studies in Creativity and Culture, DOI 10.1007/978-3-319-64577-3

The manufacturer's authorised representative in the EU is Springer Nature Customer Service Centre GmbH, Europaplatz 3, 69115 Heidelberg, Germany. If you have any concerns regarding our products, please contact ProductSafety@springernature.com

Printed and bound by CPI Group (UK) Ltd, Croydon, CR0 4YY

22/09/2026

02221067-0018